Self-Sufficient Living

Canning
and
Preserving

The Beginner's Guide to Preparing, Canning, and Storing Veggies, Fruits, Meats, and More

Adams Media

New York   London   Toronto   Sydney   New Delhi

Aadamsmedia

Adams Media
An Imprint of Simon & Schuster, Inc.
57 Littlefield Street
Avon, Massachusetts 02322

First Adams Media trade paperback edition September 2020

ADAMS MEDIA and colophon are trademarks of Simon & Schuster.

For information about special discounts for bulk purchases, please contact Simon & Schuster Special Sales at 1-866-506-1949 or business@simonandschuster.com.

The Simon & Schuster Speakers Bureau can bring authors to your live event. For more information or to book an event contact the Simon & Schuster Speakers Bureau at 1-866-248-3049 or visit our website at www.simonspeakers.com.

Interior design by Julia Jacintho
Interior illustrations by Eric Andrews

Manufactured in the United States of America

10 9 8 7 6 5 4 3 2 1

Library of Congress Cataloging-in-Publication Data has been applied for.

ISBN 978-1-5072-1461-9
ISBN 978-1-5072-1462-6 (ebook)

CONTENTS

INTRODUCTION

Are you constantly running to the grocery store just to keep your refrigerator stocked? Are you worried that you aren't prepared enough for a potential emergency? Do you feel more secure when you have a full pantry and freezer? Wouldn't it be a wonderful feeling if you knew that you had everything you needed to survive, and even thrive, at home? The more self-sufficient you become, the more possible that outcome is!

Self-sufficiency means many different things to different people. Some simply decide to install solar paneling to reduce their electricity bills. Some find self-sufficiency in backyard farms with gardens and grain storage to provide the fresh food their families need. And some may collect their own water, grow acres of crops, and tend livestock.

Let's not forget that everyone's reasoning for becoming more self-sufficient is different as well. You may decide to start a self-sufficient home because you are concerned with security. You don't feel that the world is a safe place for you and your family, and you want to take steps to be more independent and create a self-reliant lifestyle for yourself and the ones you love. Perhaps you want to save money and stop relying on big chain stores for food and supplies. Or maybe it's just as simple as lowering your carbon footprint and living a greener, eco-friendlier life.

The good news is, depending on your resources and your motivation, living self-sufficiently can be done quickly, or it can be done in a series of small steps over a period of time. The beauty of your self-sufficient home is that you get to determine what you want to do and how far you want to go. You can start by looking at your finances to see where you can economize. Chart how often you run to the grocery store, coffee shop, or fast-food restaurant, and limit your exposure to any or all of them. Look at your food preparation habits and substitute basic homemade items for convenience foods.

Whether you are prepping for an emergency or just looking to feel more empowered, canning and preserving is one of the easiest, least expensive ways to become more self-sufficient. And whether you're an experienced canner and preserver looking to broaden your skills, or you're just getting started, *Canning and Preserving* will teach you all you need to know about cooking and properly storing delicious foods for the long run. Here you'll learn how to can and preserve your fruits, vegetables, and meats and build a full pantry (or freezer) full of fresh, homemade food you can use whenever you need it. You'll also find 150 recipes ranging from gourmet jams and luscious mustards to mouthwatering marinades and pleasing pickles, as well as recipes that use these preserved goods for dinners, desserts, and more. In no time at all, you'll have enough food stored for months! Talk about self-sufficient…

CHAPTER ONE

Canning and Preserving Fundamentals

Throughout history, people have preserved their foods to last them through times of strife, to create a secure stockpile that they can trust in, or simply to enjoy the fresh and diverse flavors created by preserving. Today, having what you need on hand, immediately available if and when you need it, is becoming more and more important. Why? The security of having a full pantry and freezer full of healthy and nutritious food for you and your family, the peace-of-mind feeling of being prepared for any emergency, and the cost savings of buying and preserving in bulk are among the many benefits of preserving for self-sustainability. Throughout this chapter you'll find some background on what exactly preserving food means and the history of practicing self-sustainability through food preservation, as well as a number of basic guidelines for setting up your kitchen for canning and preserving at home.

Preservation Will Help You Become More Self-Sufficient

People whose homes are well stocked are best prepared in case disaster strikes. While you can't prepare for every circumstance, keeping a full pantry (that is almost free of spoilage concerns) is perhaps the most important aspect of being ready for any situation. Knowing you can provide for yourself and your family no matter what happens provides genuine peace of mind. In addition, market trends and resources in stores can be unpredictable, so taking charge of your own materials and supplies helps you stock your pantry on your terms. In addition, by purchasing far fewer single-use packages for ingredients and meals, you'll lower your carbon footprint considerably. The well-stocked pantry is a blessing, as is the ability to remain self-reliant.

On an individual level, you'll feel the personal pleasure and pride that comes from self-sufficiency. When people come to visit, you can offer them samplings from your stores and share the stories that go with each dish. This is how other people get inspired to preserve and how recipes get passed along from family to family and generation to generation. Next, you'll learn why canning for yourself is an important skill in today's modern world.

Why Canning Is Important

When people hear about canning projects, often their first reaction is surprise that someone would undertake such a daunting task. But people who preserve their own food want healthy, tasty meals that they created themselves—from the ground up! The benefits of food security on one's own terms far outweigh relying on mass market food stores and other unpredictable variables. While the initial process takes a little while, the end result lasts for months and requires no tinkering to perfect! Devoting a few hours on a weekend to making tomato sauce yields several jars that will last for months. In addition to the convenience of having tomato sauce at your fingertips whenever you need it, making your own sauce and other fresh and healthy necessities will save you money in the long run.

Fresh and Healthy Sustainability

There is also a freshness factor to canning. If your self-sufficiency includes your own garden, you will find this a particularly useful way to enjoy your harvest throughout the year, long after the garden has gone brown or become covered in snow. For example, the gardener with gently tended organic grapes can harvest and can them into jelly or jam on the same day and retain that treasured fresh flavor. If you grow tomatoes, you can take the fruit at the height of its ripeness, preserving its greater concentrations of vitamin C, and create all manner of rich salsas and sauces. Nothing in the commercial market comes close.

Preservation Pointers

If you're looking for high concentrations of vitamin C, trust in broccoli, red and yellow bell peppers, kohlrabi, kiwi, mango, papaya, and tomatoes. A whole mango, for example, provides more than 180 milligrams of vitamin C.

Home canning gives you a healthier option as well. Commercially preserved goods often include chemicals that aren't remotely part of an average person's working vocabulary. They also include added salt, sugar, and preserving agents, some of which cause allergic reactions. These additives are potentially harmful to people with serious health issues. Sulfates may trigger hives and aggravate asthma in people with sensitivity to this chemical. In high amounts, salt is considered a contributor to strokes and heart disease. Stockpiling these mass-produced canned goods to be eaten regularly may seem wise to those who want to be more self-reliant, but the overprocessed ingredients in them can deteriorate your health. Home preserving gives you the power to decide what to put in your body. Rather than risk eating a store-bought item that contains several overprocessed ingredients, you can make and preserve something at home that you know will be tasty and healthy, and will last you months.

You should always review the basic costs before you begin. Include the recipe ingredients, the tools and equipment you need to buy, and the gas or electricity needed to process the item. Even though preserving your own food will take longer than buying cans at the store, it's well worth the effort to have fresh and healthy food on your table.

Keeping Tradition Alive

Another reason many people preserve is to continue a family tradition. In the past, at various times of the year, children and adults alike helped prepare whatever was about to be put up for the season. Family stories were retold, and Mom's best-kept secret recipes were shared in the hopes of safeguarding them for future generations. It's only since World War II that such warm, communal scenes began to disappear from our homes. The disconnect between a family and its history, the lessened communication, and the loss of all manner of customs are just a few of the results. Many modern preservers are often looking to reconnect with that lost sense of self-sufficiency as they revive old traditions with modern safety precautions.

Food Preservation and Self-Sustainability

The ability to always have food on hand, available no matter the circumstance, was invaluable in the past and remains so today. At one time, our ancestors lived at the mercy of the harvesting and hunting seasons. The minute an animal dies or a vegetable leaves the soil, it begins to decompose. The discovery of preservation introduced the revolutionary idea that food no longer needed to be immediately consumed after foraging or hunting, ensuring a more stable lifestyle and warding off starvation. Nearly every modern idea about preserving came from the careful and creative methods of our ancestors across the globe.

They discovered various means to safely preserve their food to last through periods of hibernation, winter, drought, monsoons, and any other unforeseen circumstance. They developed methods to avoid the formation of bacteria and mold, despite the diverse range of processes and products. For example, they discovered that freezing and drying both cause a reduction in water, which deters spoiling. However, the textural result of freezing versus drying is vastly different. Likewise, heating food kills many organisms, as does soaking food in alcohol, but the resulting taste of the food is very dissimilar.

Ancient peoples may not have understood the science behind why some things lasted or why others made them ill, but they paid attention to the big picture and taught what they learned to the next generation in order to keep their families healthy and sustained. These skills, refined through time, tradition, and modern science, are just as useful and applicable today as they were thousands of years ago. Here you'll learn the history of different methods of preservation and why these methods still work to help you be more self-sufficient today.

Drying

Drying is a very effective way of preserving many foods because it decreases water, therefore thwarting or slowing any unhealthy organism's growth. Drying is best suited to meats, fruits, and grains. This form of preservation is perhaps the oldest of all methods. There is evidence that ancient peoples dried food as long ago as 12,000 B.C.E., especially in the Middle East. Trade routes helped spread the use of this method, along with a healthy bit of folklore, especially regarding dried herbs. By the time the Roman Empire was founded, buildings were created for drying herbs, fruits, and vegetables. When sun was lacking, fire was used instead. When people could keep stores of dried foods in their homes, livelihood improved, leading to the success of the Roman Empire.

Fermentation

Most historians consider the discovery of fermentation an accidental wonder. There's no question that the art of brewing was known to the ancient Sumerians by around 10,000 B.C.E., more than likely because a bit of bread was left in water too long. The first fermented beverages were venerated as divine in origin, especially when people found that drinking this brew was often healthier than drinking water. Over time, people moved beyond fermenting beverages and began fermenting foods as well. Studies indicate that foods can develop more vitamins as they ferment, creating a healthier end product.

Various cultures buried foods as a type of fermenting method. Examples include eggs in China, shark in Iceland, kimchi in Korea, and rice-bran pickles in Japan. Fermenting can make a toxic item like raw cassava root safely consumable.

Pickling

Pickling preserves food by the use of brine (a liquid with high salt content) mixed with vinegar, alcohol, or oil. Pickling usually applies heat somewhere along the way so the food accepts the brine until the point of saturation. This also improves flavor! Nearly all vegetables are well suited to pickling.

Pickling has been popular for at least four thousand years. Pickles as we know them were developed in India and Babylon around 2000 B.C.E. and quickly spread to other parts of the world. Once this tasty sensation hit Rome, there was no stopping it. Romans even used the brine from pickles for fish sauce, doubling the use of their stores. The first containers for pickling were made of stoneware, which effectively increased their shelf life, as the acid content in the brine could dissolve a less hearty clay pot.

Smoking

Smoking offers a twofold benefit: It preserves food using heat and smoke, which also gives it extra flavor. Many people who grill enjoy using a variety of wood for smoking to achieve different tastes and aromas. Meat, poultry, and fish are the three most predominantly smoked items. Some nuts are also commonly smoked.

It's difficult to pinpoint exactly when people began to smoke food in order to keep it longer. We do know that the Roman world loved sausage, which was likely smoked for longevity. Smoking was also popular in the Middle Ages, especially for fish such as cod and herring. Those who lived far from the coast could then purchase and stockpile smoked coastal fish.

Typically, these fish were smoked for about 3 weeks before they were ready for transport. On the other side of the world, Native Americans were cutting, seasoning, and smoking various meats for storage, creating vast stockpiles for entire tribes.

Freezing

Freezing is one of the most utilized preserving processes. Items have a very long shelf life when properly packed, wrapped, and frozen.

The first documented ice cellars appear in China around 1000 B.C.E., and the Greeks and Romans used a similar method to preserve their food. However, it wasn't until the 1800s that refrigeration as we know it came into popular use.

Preservation Pointers

Freezer burn is caused by dehydration in foods that aren't properly wrapped and packaged. The food often looks lighter in color, and the flavor or texture is likely to have been altered slightly. Experts recommend using vacuum sealing and other moisture-resistant packaging methods to avoid freezer burn. Always eat the items that have been in your freezer the longest first.

Sugaring

The Greeks and Romans preserved foods with sugar and honey. One favorite method was to press fruit into jars with the chosen sweetener, but meats could be preserved with honey and sugar as well. The Romans also used various spices such as coriander to preserve foods.

Most commonly seen in the preservation of fruit, sugar may be combined with water to create syrup or alcohol. Additionally, sugar may be crystallized on a fruit or spice to create a protective coating, as in candied ginger.

Jellying

There are a variety of items that create a jelly-type base for preserving, including fruit pectin, gelatin, and arrowroot flour. After jellying, the resulting food is often canned for increased longevity.

If you're planning on making your jams, jellies, and other preserved products into a sideline business, do your research. You may need a food permit or a totally separate kitchen for preparation to comply with state laws. Check your local ordinances regarding zoning, and don't forget things like state tax permits and insurance.

Canning

Canning begins with good food and sterile jars. It's very important that the storage containers used in canning are properly cleaned to kill bacteria. Additionally, canning includes hot-water baths (for high-acid items) and pressure canning (for low-acid items) to create a vacuum and kill off any lingering, potentially harmful microbes, specifically botulinum, which has no odor or taste and causes the potentially deadly food poisoning known as botulism.

The 1800s saw the development of canning at the turn of the century, when a confectioner named Nicolas Appert applied heat to sealed glass bottles for the French navy. Canning tins came about in 1810, and in 1863 the renowned scientist Louis Pasteur explained why these preservation processes helped prevent illness. However, the process really took off during World War II, when canned edibles were needed for the troops. During the war, the popularity of Victory Gardens gave rise to home canning efforts. The goal was to decrease the amount of food a household needed to buy so that commercially canned edibles, which were rationed, could go to the troops. About 40 percent of household consumable fruits and vegetables were preserved from these gardens until the late 1940s.

Now that you know the basics and the history behind each preservation method, you'll need to know some basic safety guidelines as you work toward self-sustainability.

Guidelines for Self-Sufficiency Beginners

Let's take a look at some basic guidelines that will help keep the food you and your family are storing safe and long-lasting. These guidelines are generalized toward all preserving efforts, especially for people who are new to the art. Even if you have been preserving for a while, though, take a peek to jog your memory. Sometimes we get into bad habits or forget some of the basics that are so important to positive results. Touchstones like this will help.

Preservation Pointers

Canned goods require a cool, dark, and dry place for storage. The recommended temperature is between 50°F and 70°F. Under these conditions, your canned goods will last about a year. Temperatures greater than 90°F and exposure to direct sunlight dramatically decrease safe storage time.

The following are some strategies for successful preserving:

- Learn one method first. Pick out one preserving method that really appeals to you and get a good handle on it before launching into another one. This yields better results than if you split your attention and budget.

- Have a game plan for your projects. Why are you preserving? How much do you need to preserve to keep up with your household and keep enough product available when you need it in the future? How much is feasible based on your schedule? Set dates based on your demands and time constraints.

- Set a reasonable goal with a specific focus. For example, make one or two types of jelly in one weekend. Focus on sauce another weekend.

- Start out small. Small batches of everything tend to work better in preserving. You don't need to learn everything overnight. Take your time and really gain expertise. Start clean and end clean.

- Have a functional sitting/working area. If there's going to be a long round of peeling or chopping, you'll really want that chair!

- Keep measurements tight and recipes come out right! Some preserving recipes require very specific components to work correctly.

- Adhere to the processing times provided in recipes. These are necessary to deter microbe growth. If you're not sure, check the information against USDA guidelines.

- Know your audience. If you're preserving for other people, make sure you're aware of their personal tastes and allergies. When people ask for the same thing twice, those are your winners!

- Write it down! When you adapt a recipe and it works right, document your process and keep it in a safe place for future reference.

- Label and date everything. This provides you with a visual gauge for shelf life and distinguishes a red, sweet, gooey thing from a red, spicy-hot thing.

- Keep track of your stock. Keep a running list of what you have in your storage pantry so you can plan meals and future preservation efforts. Remember, you only want to store enough for about a year's consumption from a safety perspective.

- Have the right tools for the job and follow the manufacturer's instructions for those tools. Each section in this book will outline the necessary tools so you can budget accordingly.

- Use the highest quality ingredients your budget will allow. Investing a little more in your components will result in far healthier, longer-lasting items.

- Create adequate space for your preserving projects. You need enough space for your tools and ingredients and the resulting products. Get creative. For example, an old wooden crate can transform into perfect shelving for a cellar!

- When in doubt, throw it out! Never take chances with your health. If something seems off, it probably is.

- Finally, seek out others in your area or on the Internet who share your passion. Exchange ideas. Talk about those utter failures and amazing successes so that everyone benefits. Share recipes and advice. Taste test among your family and ask for feedback. This is a wonderful way to perfect recipes and improve your skills at the same time.

CHAPTER TWO

Canning

Canning is one of the more modern forms of preserving food. Its ease of use and practicality lend as much to self-sustainability in our modern world as ancient methods of sun drying or freezing foods in the snow did. The ability to can allows you to creatively and safely preserve your favorite foods and fill up your pantry shelves entirely on your own, outside of grocery stores and mass manufacturing. While eating store-bought canned meals regularly is frowned upon because of all the unhealthy chemical additives used to preserve them, canning your own food is a simple solution that gives you the power and independence to preserve with healthy, wholesome, and cost-efficient ingredients. If you're nervous about canning food, know that the processes used today are very safe when you follow the directions carefully. This chapter will detail the types of canning and the implements you'll need to start canning for self-sustainability.

Water-Bath or Pressure Canner?

The most important piece of equipment for canning is the canner itself, but a lot of people don't know what type of canner to get or when to use pressure canning versus a water-bath method. The simple rule of thumb is that all high-acid foods go into a water-bath canner, and everything else must be processed in a pressure canner. High-acid foods are all fruit products (jams, jellies, preserves, conserves, fruit butters, and marmalades) and anything pickled with vinegar, like pickles, relishes, and vinegar-based sauces. The water-bath canner increases the temperature in the canning jar enough to kill bacteria, and it also pushes out air bubbles as the content expands. As the jars cool, the air pressure creates the seal that makes the lid pop.

Water-bath canners are made of aluminum or porcelain-covered steel. They have removable perforated racks and fitted lids. The canner must be deep enough so that at least 1" of briskly boiling water will be over the tops of the jars during processing. Some water-bath canners do not have flat bottoms, which are essential for use on an electric range. Either a flat or ridged bottom can be used on a gas burner. To ensure uniform processing of all jars with an electric range, the diameter of the canner should be no more than 4" inches wider than the element on which it is heated.

Look for a water-bath canner that has a rack for the jars so they don't clank together during boiling. Some home preservers use a large stockpot and a homemade rack system, but department stores offer very affordable water-bath canning kits starting at around $30.

For low-acid foods, you'll need a pressure cooker. Low-acid foods are all nonpickled vegetables, meat, fish, poultry, and dried beans. The pressure cooker gets much hotter than a hot-water canner (250°F), and it maintains that heat throughout processing to kill any microbes. Notice there's no mention of tomatoes here. That's because tomatoes (which are fruits) can be processed in either a water-bath canner or a pressure cooker. In either case, lemon juice must be added to tomatoes to raise the acidity level.

For those who want to be self-sustainable across a range of different foods, consider buying the pressure canner, as it easily becomes a water-bath canner just by leaving the lid off. As you become more familiar with canning, you'll be able to use the pressure canner to fill your pantry with more diverse choices than by choosing a water-bath canner. The pressure canner can also be used for other culinary efforts, such as tenderizing cheap cuts of meat.

Buying Guide

Home-use pressure canners have been extensively redesigned in recent years. Models made before the 1970s were heavy-walled kettles with clamp-on or turn-on lids. They were fitted with a dial gauge, a vent port in the form of a petcock or counterweight, and a safety fuse. Modern pressure canners, which cost about $100 for a 10-to-16-quart size, are lightweight, thin-walled kettles; most have turn-on lids. They have a jar rack, a gasket, a dial or weighted gauge, an automatic vent/cover lock, a vent port (steam vent) to be closed with a counterweight or weighted gauge, and a safety fuse.

Tools of the Trade

The following is a list of the basic canning equipment a self-sustainable canner will need to operate. Now is the time to take an inventory of your canning supplies and equipment and start gathering screw bands, lids, and jars so that you can stock your own pantry as you see fit. If your pressure canner uses a rubber gasket, get a pair of them. If a gasket blows in the middle of a canning project, you'll need the replacement right at your fingertips.

Basic Canning Equipment

- Water-bath canner (You can use a large stockpot with a lid. Any pot used as a water-bath canner must have a rack to keep the jars off the bottom.)

- Pressure canner if you intend to stock vegetables, meats, and nonacidic products in your pantry

- Canning jars—Mason jars in pint, quart, and jelly (half-pint) sizes

- Lids and rings

- Large spoons for mixing and stirring

- Metal soup ladles

- Sharp paring knives

- Vegetable peeler

- Canning funnel

- Colander and/or large strainer

- Large slotted spoons

- Measuring cups and spoons

- Squeezer or juicer

- Food mill, food processor, and/or blender
- Canning-jar lifter and lid wand

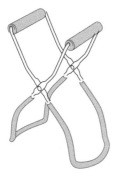

- Plastic spatula or other stirrer for getting air bubbles out of jars
- Kitchen timer

- Cheesecloth for making spice balls or large tea balls
- Canning and pickling salt, Fruit-Fresh, powdered and liquid fruit pectin, and CLEARJEL
- Kitchen towels
- Aprons
- Disposable food-preparation gloves
- Long-handled jar scrubber
- Kitchen scale
- Jelly bags
- Zester, mandoline, melon baller, apple peeler, and cherry pitter

Jars, Lids, and Screw Bands

Only Mason jars are safe for canning. Commercial jars like those used for mayonnaise and peanut butter were designed for one-time use only. They may crack or shatter in either a water-bath or a pressure canner. While the old bail-wire jars look pretty, they are no longer recommended for canning. Save the antique jars for storage purposes.

Half-Pint Mason Jar   **Pint Mason Jar**   **Quart Mason Jar**

Use canning jars in sizes suitable for the product and your family's needs as you anticipate how far in advance you are stockpiling, according to safety recommendations. Canning jars generally are sold in half-pint, pint, and quart sizes with wide and regular mouths. Wide-mouth jars are convenient for packing such foods as whole tomatoes and peach halves. Quart jars work well for vegetables and fruits if your family has four or more members. Consider the size of your pantry, and how many cans you need to have on hand for you and your family.

As you consider different preservation methods, and plan ahead for you and your family, you may want to calculate how much to can for one person to use in a year. For the average person, a good canning goal for self-sufficiency is about 140 quarts of fruits and vegetables, 36 pints of meat, 18 quarts of soup, 20 pints of spreads, 5 pints of relish, and 26 pints of various types of pickles! These numbers may vary depending on your preferences, ages, and dietary restrictions, and canning all these materials at once would be nearly impossible, but it is very achievable given time and good planning.

Some commercial pasta sauces are packaged in Mason jars. Note, however, that they are not a full quart. If you decide to reuse these, make absolutely certain that the screw band fits it perfectly, as the threading on some jars does not match that of the commercially available screw bands.

If you have extra unused lids, store them protected in a dry, cool place. A Rubbermaid storage box with a tight-fitting lid works quite well for storage of extra lids and screw bands. The US Department of Agriculture does not recommend reusing lids because there is a chance they may not seal properly. Before storing used screw bands, wash them in hot soapy water, dry them well, and put them into your storage container.

Preparation

Before you start canning, read your recipe at least twice and assemble your ingredients. Don't buy all the ingredients to stockpile your pantry at once, as they'll most likely spoil before you have the time to preserve them all. Organize the supplies and equipment you will need to complete your project one at a time. Learning you are out of a certain ingredient in the middle of a canning session is not fun! Also remember: Canning projects require your uninterrupted attention from start to finish.

Next, prepare your workspace. This is where you will be preparing the food as you work toward self-sustainability. Clear the kitchen counters so you have ample space to work. You need counter space for preparing your foods as well as space for filling your jars once the food is prepared.

Determine how many jars your recipe calls for. Examine the jars carefully, making certain there are no cracks or chips. You may put them through a sterilizing cycle in a dishwasher if you have one. Otherwise, use a bottle brush to scrub them inside and out, rinse them in hot water, and sterilize them in a large stockpot or water-bath canner. Meanwhile, your lids should be placed in a bowl of hot water to soften the rubber sealing compound.

Preservation Pointers

When filling jars, place an old terrycloth bath towel folded in half or two terrycloth kitchen towels on your counter. Never put jars on an uncovered countertop. Putting a jar on an uncovered surface and then filling it with hot food and/or liquid may cause the jar or countertop to crack or shatter.

When you fill your jars, remember to leave the proper amount of headspace—¼" for jams, jellies, preserves, and most other water bath–processed foods, and 1" for pressure-processed foods. Each recipe will specify the amount of necessary headspace. You may be tempted to fill the jars as much as you can to maximize your food preservation, but too little headspace may cause liquid to seep out. If there's too much head-space, food at the top of the jar may dry out.

Finally, remove air bubbles from the jar. This can be accomplished by gently stirring the contents of the jar with a plastic spatula or other stirrer (a wide plastic soda straw works great). Use a damp kitchen towel to wipe the outer rims, then put on a lid and screw the band firmly. Do not over-tighten screw bands. Doing so may cause the lids to buckle in the canner.

Processing

In a water bath, jars are placed on a rack and covered with 1"–2" boiling water. Put a lid on the bath and begin timing when the water is boil-ing. When finished, remove the jars with a jar lifter and place them on a towel-covered counter to cool. Leave them undisturbed for 12–24 hours. Check the seals and remove the screw bands. Doing so allows you to reuse the screw bands and prevents them from rusting or being difficult to remove when the jar is opened.

Preservation Pointers

The old computer expression GIGO (Garbage In = Garbage Out) applies to home canning as well. Your finished pantry is only as good as the ingredients you begin with. Be sure to stockpile your pantry with freshly picked fruits and vegetables for preserving, because the sooner you jar fresh ingredients, the better. Canning will not improve stale foodstuffs.

In a pressure canner, jars are placed on a rack and boiling water is added according to the manufacturer's instructions, usually several inches. Lock the lid securely into place. Leave the weight off the vent pipe or open the petcock and exhaust the steam for 10 minutes. Place the weight back onto the vent pipe or close the petcock. The canner should start to pressurize in 5–10 minutes. Once the canner has reached the required level of pressure, start the timer. Allow the canner to come down to 0 pounds on its own. Do not try to speed up this process by removing weight or opening the petcock, as it may cause the jars to crack and/or lose liquid. Do not put the canner into cold water to hasten the process. Let the jars sit in the canner for 5–10 minutes to allow them to cool down. Then remove the jars with a jar lifter and place them on a towel-covered counter to cool. Leave them undisturbed for 12–24 hours. Check the seals and remove the screw bands.

Preservation Pointers

To check the seals on cooled jars, press your thumb in the middle of the lid. If the lid seems to give and come back up, the jar isn't sealed. If you're not sure, tap the lid with a knife in the same place. It should sound like a bell; a muffled sound means the jar isn't sealed right. Finally, there's the visual test—the surface of the lid should be concave.

What happens if your jar doesn't seal properly? All is not lost! You have several options here. One is to put the jar in the refrigerator and use it soon. The second is to try reprocessing the jar within 24 hours of the original effort. If you're going to do this, open the jar, make sure the lid has a clean surface, try changing out the lid, and put everything back in your canner. Your third and fourth options are using other preservation methods covered in this book, namely freezing or drying, if practicable.

After Processing

Wash off all your sealed and cooled jars, label them with the date of canning, and move them into a suitable storage place. Use your canned goods within one year unless otherwise specified by the recipe. Write expiration dates on your jars to remind you how long they will remain good. As you stock your own pantry, make sure that your jars are organized so that the oldest ones are in the front as you make use of your preserves. To prevent spoiling, keep your jars away from places that are too hot or damp, and don't expose them to bright light.

When you use your canned goods, always check for signs of spoilage. The most obvious sign is the loss of a vacuum seal on the jar and mold growing inside. Other indicators include gas bubbles, odd coloring, and foul smells. Never test suspect food—throw it out!

Safe Temperatures for Canning

At sea level, water boils at 212°F. This is the processing temperature for all high-acid and pickled foods. It is the temperature at which molds, yeasts, and some bacteria are destroyed.

Low-acid, nonpickled foods are processed in a pressure canner at 250°F. It is the temperature at which bacterial spores (botulinum) are destroyed. Botulinum, the bacterium that causes botulism, is odorless, colorless, and tasteless. In the case of an otherwise healthy adult, botulism mimics flu symptoms. In the case of a small child, an elderly adult, or a person with an impaired immune system, it may be fatal.

What Is Botulism?

Botulism is a rare but serious paralytic illness caused by a nerve toxin that is produced by the bacterium *Clostridium botulinum*. Foodborne botulism is caused by eating foods that contain the botulism toxin. Contracting botulism is a potentially fatal medical emergency.

The classic symptoms of botulism include double vision, blurred vision, drooping eyelids, slurred speech, difficulty swallowing, dry mouth, and muscle weakness. Infants with botulism appear lethargic, feed poorly, are constipated, and have a weak cry and poor muscle tone. These are all symptoms of the muscle paralysis caused by the bacterial toxin. If untreated, these symptoms may progress to cause paralysis of the arms, legs, trunk, and respiratory muscles. In food-borne botulism, symptoms generally begin 18–36 hours after eating a contaminated food, but they can occur in as soon as 6 hours or as late as 10 days.

Botulism can be prevented. Food-borne botulism has often been contracted from home-canned foods with low acid content, such as asparagus, green beans, beets, and corn. Follow strict hygienic procedures to reduce the risk of contamination. Oils infused with garlic or herbs should be refrigerated. Potatoes that have been baked while wrapped in aluminum foil should be kept hot until served or refrigerated.

Also pay close attention to the canning instructions given in this or any canning guide. Extensive instructions on safe home canning can be obtained from county extension services or from the USDA (www.usda.gov).

How Common Is Botulism?

In the United States, an average of 110 cases of botulism are reported each year. Of these, approximately 25 percent are food-borne, 72 percent are infant botulism, and the rest are wound botulism. Outbreaks of food-borne botulism involving two or more persons occur in most years and are usually caused by eating contaminated home-canned foods.

The Importance of Altitude

Do you know how high you are above sea level? You'll need to find out for canning. Water boils at different temperatures depending on your altitude. The higher you live, the lower the boiling point. This means that processing time has to be increased to offset the lower temperature, or you'll have to opt for a pressure canner. Recipes throughout this book are set for altitudes under 1,000 feet. For levels over 1,000 feet, use the following charts.

Altitude Chart for Boiling – Water Canner	
Feet above Sea Level	**Increase Processing Time By**
1,001–3,000	5 minutes
3,001–6,000	10 minutes
6,001–8,000	15 minutes
8,001–10,000	20 minutes

Altitude Chart – Pressure Canner		
Feet above Sea Level	**Weighted Gauge**	**Dial Gauge**
0–1,000	10 pounds	11 pounds
1,001–2,000	15 pounds	11 pounds
2,001–3,000	15 pounds	12 pounds
3,001–6,000	15 pounds	13 pounds
6,001–8,000	15 pounds	14 pounds
8,001–10,000	15 pounds	15 pounds

What Not to Can

As you stock your pantry for the weeks, months, and year ahead, know that you cannot can everything you are used to having. Anything containing pasta, rice, and barley cannot be canned safely. These low-acid ingredients common to soups, stews, and other convenience meals need to be pressure processed at length. During this time they break down and may, in fact, make the foodstuff too dense for the heat to safely kill the botulism spores.

Second, any dairy products like eggs, milk, cream, cheese, and butter are not safe to can. You can make pickled eggs and refrigerate them, but they need to be used within 2 weeks. Oils also aren't good candidates. While flavored oils can be made for short-term use, oils generally get rancid very quickly.

Anything high in fat doesn't can well. Excess fat should be removed from meat, and ground beef should be sautéed and drained of excess fat. Allow soups and stocks to cool, skim the fat off, and then reheat and process them. Like oils, fat tends to go rancid.

Last but not least, don't can anything thickened with flour, cornstarch, arrowroot, or bread crumbs. CLEARJEL, which is a modified cornstarch, may be used for safely canning pie fillings but is not safe for thickening sauces or gravies.

Equipment and Methods Not Recommended for Home Canning

On your journey toward self-sustainability, you may want to make use of the equipment and appliances that you already have to preserve your food. However, processing freshly filled jars in conventional ovens, microwave ovens, and dishwashers is not recommended, because these practices do not prevent all risks of spoilage. The following list details other methods of canning and preserving to avoid.

- Steam canners. Processing times for use with current models have not been adequately researched. Steam canners may not heat foods in the same manner as water-bath canners, so this could require changing processing times. Without clear guidelines, food spoilage may result.

- Pressure processes in excess of 15 PSI, especially when using new pressure-canning equipment. Most manufacturers also do not recommend operating their pressure canners above 15 PSI.

- Canning powders. These are not preservatives. You still need to properly process your canned goods.

- Jars with wire bails and glass caps. While these make attractive antiques or storage containers for dry food ingredients, they're not recommended for use in canning.

- Using old lids (even unused ones). The longer a lid sits, the more likely it is that it won't seal correctly. Don't purchase more lids than you anticipate using in a year.

- One-piece zinc, porcelain-lined caps. These are no longer recommended. Both glass and zinc caps use flat rubber rings for sealing jars, but the zinc caps fail to seal properly.

Help and Hints

All steps of any canning project should be carried through as rapidly as possible. As you work on a canning project, follow the slogan, "Two hours from harvest to container." Work quickly with small amounts of food at a time, especially vegetables with a high starch content that lose their quality rapidly, such as corn and peas. If you decide to dedicate an afternoon to work on canning and stockpiling, make sure you refrigerate any food items you won't be using within 2 hours. Set reasonable expectations for your work, because any delay will result in loss of flavor and nutritive value in your canned products. Additionally, following these simple rules will make your efforts more successful and satisfying:

- Use prime products; discard any parts with defects.

- Keep same-sized items together in jars for even processing.

- Wash tools and ingredients thoroughly. Be fastidious!

- Always set jars on a rack in the bottom of your canner to avoid breakage and ensure water circulation. Do not use a folded towel; this is not safe.

- Follow up-to-date recommendations for detailed procedures in canning, available in USDA or extension publications. Check for updates and new recommendations regularly.

Finally, have fun! While the rules sound like drudgery, they're really not difficult. With just a little practice, you'll find the preparations and mechanisms come quite naturally—and you'll have a plethora of wonderful, self-sustainable canned goods to fill your pantry with.

CHAPTER THREE

Freezing for Self-Sustainability

With the invention of the home refrigerator and freezer at the beginning of the twentieth century, food preservation has become so commonplace that most people don't think twice about freezing anything. Freezing and refrigeration are the most common types of preserving in homes around the world today, but many don't consider it a resource that could prove vital in an emergency. The ability to stock one's freezer is an act of self-sustainability even if the products within weren't all self-preserved. As freezer space is limited, and freezers themselves can be costly, you'll want to make the most of your freezer by stocking up on healthy, sustainable meals that you'll make. The difference between the ultra-processed, pre-packaged freezer meals you'll find at the grocery store versus the nutritious meals you can freeze on your own is truly astounding. As you'll learn in this chapter, freezing healthy ingredients and meals for you and your family is extremely accessible, and when done correctly, it's one of your greatest assets for self-sustainability.

Freezing Fundamentals

Whereas refrigeration slows bacterial action, freezing comes close to totally stopping microbes' development. This happens because the water in frozen food turns to ice, in which bacteria cannot continue to grow. Enzyme activity, on the other hand, isn't completely deterred by freezing, which is why many vegetables are blanched before being packaged. Once an item is defrosted completely, however, any microbes still within will begin to grow again.

Except for eggs in the shell, nearly all foods can be frozen after blanching and/or cooking. So the real question here is which foods don't take well to freezing. The following list includes the foods you generally cannot freeze:

- Cream sauces separate even when warmed completely after being frozen.
- Mayonnaise, cream cheese, and cottage cheese don't hold up well, often losing textural quality.
- Milk seems to be a fifty-fifty proposition. While it can be frozen quite safely, it sometimes separates after being frozen. If remixed, this milk is an option for cooking and baking.
- Precooked meat can be frozen, but it doesn't have as much moisture as raw meat and will often dry out further if left frozen more than 4 weeks.
- Cured meats don't last long in the freezer and should be used in less than 4 weeks.

If you're in doubt about how to best prepare an item for freezing (or even if you should), the *National Center for Home Food Preservation* (https://nchfp.uga.edu) is a great resource. It offers tips on how to freeze various items, ranging from pie and prepared food to oysters and artichokes.

Preservation Pointers

The ideal temperature for keeping foods frozen for the longest time without losing textural or taste quality is 0°F (18°C). Before buying a freezer, check to see that it achieves that temperature, if not colder.

Frosty Facts

As you stock your freezer full of healthy meals, remember that zero is your magic number. At 0°F, microbes become dormant. Your stockpiled food won't spoil, and any germs therein will not breed until you defrost the food. Bear in mind, though, that the longer the food remains frozen the more it tends to lose certain qualities such as vivid flavor and texture. Be sure that you are always using your frozen food in an appropriate amount of time, and then freezing fresh food to replace your frozen stockpile. Always try to freeze things when they're at their peak, and remember that cooking your defrosted food as soon as it's thawed will also stop microbial growth.

Preservation Pointers

The faster food freezes, the fewer ice crystals will form. This is especially important for meat, which loses juiciness and tenderness as a result of freezing. If your freezer has a quick-freeze cycle, use that to help deter ice crystal formation. Otherwise, just wrap and seal your foods properly and put them in the coldest part of your freezer.

The first step in freezing for self-sustainability is keeping your items cold until you're ready to prepare them. This is very important with meat, but it also makes a difference in how fruits and vegetables come out of the freezer. You'll want your stockpiled frozen food to be as similar to the fresh version as possible when defrosted to make the most of your sustained stockpile.

Equipment

Once you're ready to begin, assemble all the items you need. For example, if you're freezing fruit, you'll want a clean cutting board, a sharp knife, and appropriate storage containers. Make sure that the containers are able to stack well in your freezer so that you can maximize freezer space for your stockpile. If you're doing any preparation of the fruit before freezing it, you'll also need cooking pans. Stainless steel is highly recommended; galvanized pans may give off zinc when fruit is left in them because of the fruit's acid content. Additionally, there's nothing like stainless steel for easy cleanup.

If it's in your budget, a vacuum sealer is another great piece of equipment to consider for self-sustainability. Vacuum sealers come in a variety of sizes with a similar variety of bags that are perfect for preservers who like freezing and drying methods. They cut down on wasted space in the freezer as you fill the space, and they're  fairly cost effective when compared to freezer bags or plastic containers. Most important, they eliminate the excess air that contributes to ice crystals.

A final item that you shouldn't be without is a freezer-proof label system. If you double-wrap your frozen items, put a label on each layer. If one gets knocked off, the other remains. Use the labels to write down expiration dates so that you and your family can use items and replace them regularly.

Help and Hints

Freezing, like any other method of preservation, requires some observation and annotation to achieve success. As you're working with recipes, remember that practice really does make perfect. For example, you may follow a recipe for frozen butter pickles exactly the first time, but you find using different materials and ingredients gives you fresher and more sustainable end products the second time. Make a note of that and change the recipe accordingly.

As you note changes you'd like to make, also consider if that means getting different types of equipment for your kitchen. You'll want to invest in the equipment that best enhances your ability to stock your freezer with the most wholesome, healthy meals and ingredients. In the case of cucumbers and other thinly sliced vegetables, a mandoline might be the perfect fix. Put it on a wish list. Being prepared is the key to self-sustainability, and having the right tools is always a great boon.

Vegetables

Vegetables should be chosen for crispness and freshness. Home gardeners should pick their items a few hours before packing them for the ultimate in organic goodness. Check your garden daily for maximum ripeness, and be sure to use the frozen ingredients in your freezer as you pack more in order to maximize your freezer space. Before you freeze your vegetables, though, you'll need to understand blanching, which will improve the lifespan of your frozen goods.

Blanching

Blanching has several benefits. It stops enzyme action that decreases vegetables' textural quality, flavor, and color, and it cleans off any lingering dirt. To blanch vegetables, fill a saucepan with water and bring it to a rolling boil. Add the vegetables and make sure they're fully immersed. Follow the blanching time recommended in the recipes in this book, and then empty the vegetables into a bowl of ice water. This helps the vegetables retain their vitamins and firmness.

If there's no specific blanching time provided in your preserving recipe, here's a brief overview to get you started. Remember to move your vegetables into an ice bath immediately after blanching until they're totally cooled.

Timing and Techniques for Blanching Vegetables

- **Asparagus.** Remove the tough ends from the asparagus. Depending on the storage container and how you plan to fill your freezer space, you may need to cut the stems in half. If your stalks are thin, they'll only need 2 minutes of blanching; thick stalks require twice as much.

- **Beans (green or wax).** Remove any tips. Leave the beans whole and blanch for 3 minutes.

- **Brussels sprouts.** Remove the outer leaves, then soak the sprouts in cold salt water for 30 minutes. Drain and blanch for 4 minutes.

- **Cabbage.** Remove the outer leaves. Shred the cabbage and blanch for just over 1 minute. Remove from the heat but leave the cabbage in the water for another 30 seconds before icing.

- **Carrots.** Clean the skins, then slice into ¼" pieces. Blanch for 3 minutes. Whole baby carrots need 5 minutes of blanching.

- **Cauliflower and broccoli.** Break off the pieces from the central core and clean well (a spray nozzle at the sink works very well). Soak for 30 minutes in a gallon of water to which 3–4 teaspoons salt have been added. Pour off the salt water. Rinse and blanch for 3 minutes.

- **Corn.** Rinse, remove from the cob, and blanch for 5 minutes.

- **Greens (including spinach).** Rinse. Remove any leaves that have spots or other damage. Blanch for 3 minutes.

- **Herbs.** Rinse sprigs. Blanch for 2–3 seconds. Remove from water when the color of the leaves is noticeably brighter green.

- **Mushrooms (small).** These can be frozen whole. Toss with a little fresh lemon juice and blanch for 4 minutes.

- **Peas.** Remove from the husk and blanch for 90 seconds.

- **Peas in the pod.** Trim the ends and remove strings. Blanch for 1–2 minutes, depending on the size of the pod.

- **Peppers.** Slice open and remove the seeds. Cut into desired size and blanch for 2 minutes.

- **Potatoes.** Wash and scrub thoroughly. Peel and blanch for 4 minutes.

- **Tomatoes.** To easily peel the skins, use a slotted spoon to dip the tomatoes in boiling water for 30 seconds. Peel and remove the core. These can be frozen whole or diced to desired size.

- **Zucchini and squash.** Peel. Cut into ½" slices and blanch for 3 minutes.

Fruit

Freeze small batches of fruit at a time so they don't brown while you're packing. Keep any fruits that you aren't immediately working on in the refrigerator to maximize their freshness. Fruit need not be packed in syrup, but many people do prefer the texture and taste that sugar or sugar syrup adds to frozen fruit. In any case, small fruits such as berries take well to a simple sprinkling. Larger chunks such as peaches do well in syrup. The average ratio is $\frac{1}{2}$ cup syrup to every pint of fruit. To maximize the longevity of your frozen fruit stock, you may want to use ascorbic acid to improve the quality. Adding about $\frac{1}{2}$ teaspoon ascorbic acid per pint is sufficient; just mix it into the syrup or a little water.

Packaging

Since 95 percent of American homes freeze some of their food regularly, it's not surprising to find people have a lot of questions on the best type of storage containers to use for self-sustainability and how to prepare food for the table after it's been frozen. Resealable plastic freezer bags are the most common receptacles, and they work well for stacking and filling your freezer space, as do freezer-safe plastic containers. While stockpiling your frozen food stock, make sure you avoid glass. While some people have been known to use glass, this is risky since the glass may crack and break when the food inside expands in the freezing process. Additionally, slippery glass jars coming out of the freezer are easily dropped.

In general as you freeze your sustained food stock, choose bags and containers that are rated well for freezing. Avoid using waxed cartons; they don't retain the food's quality as well as you'll need for maximal sustainability, and the defrosted food often becomes limp and unstable for handling. Your stockpile of packaging materials should also be resistant to leaks and oils, and all packing materials should be able to withstand freezing.

Size Counts

Another consideration is the size of your containers. Think about how many people you plan to serve, and choose freezing containers accordingly. Many who stock frozen food for self-sustainability put several servings in one large container. Make sure you separate them with a piece of aluminum foil or plastic wrap so you can take out one at a time fairly easily.

Space Constraints

While packing ingredients and meals into containers, always leave a little room for expansion. You may be tempted to stuff the food into the container to maximize your stockpile, but be conscious of temperature changes. Let the food reach room temperature before you freeze it (right out of the ice bath is a perfect time for vegetables). Putting warm or hot food in the freezer creates a temperature variance for all the food inside the freezer.

Most important, remember to label and date everything in your freezer stockpile. This will help you gauge what should be eaten first so it retains the greatest quality.

Wrap It Up

Many self-sustainable preservers wrap meat with aluminum foil or freezer wrap, then transfer it into another freezer bag or container. This decreases the chance that ice crystals will form and protects the foil from being accidentally torn. Note, however, that waxed paper isn't a good choice for freezing because it doesn't resist moisture.

Preservation Pointers

Fruit has a lot of water, meaning the faster you freeze it, the less mushy it will be when you defrost it. If your freezer goes to −10°F, that's an ideal temperature for freezing fresh fruit. Self-sustainable preservers often use lemon juice, citric acid, and ascorbic acid to maximize freshness and minimize browning. Lightly steaming the fruit before freezing also prevents browning.

Stews and Leftovers

Many people who freeze for self-sustainability regularly set aside some of what they are cooking for the freezer so they are constantly adding to their stockpile. When doing this, it's a good idea to leave food a little undercooked. Freeze the goods as soon as they reach room temperature. When you thaw it, you will finish the cooking process and can also doctor the flavor a bit at that time. Frozen foods need not be defrosted before you start cooking them. Just remember to get all the packing materials off the item first—you would not be the first person to forget this step and find unpleasant paper or wrapping in a serving of meat!

Preservation Pointers

Even after working with your self-sustained meat stockpile for a while, always be sure to read USDA labels. This label provides valuable information about freezing and cooking for safety. For example, some poultry products require that you cook them from the frozen state, while others can be defrosted. An educated consumer is a strong advocate for family health.

Safe Storage Times

The good news for those who stock for self-sustainability is that frozen food can be kept nearly indefinitely at 0°F or colder. Nonetheless, the longer the food stays frozen, the more nutrients are lost, and the greater the likelihood that ice crystals will form and decrease the overall color, taste, or textural quality of the product. Consume your frozen food regularly while continuing to replenish the stockpile as you become self-sufficient. Use simple rotation in your freezer and diligently arrange your shelves so that the oldest items are in front, and newly preserved items are in the back of the freezer. Keep in mind that the amount of time foods can be safely kept frozen decreases with temperature fluctuation in your freezer, including the variations caused by opening the door to put food in or take it out. The longer you leave the door open, the greater the temperature will change, and the more it will affect the food stored inside.

Here's a quick overview of suggested storage times for various common pantry items. More information about storage will typically be noted in the recipes you're using for freezing. Longer lists are also available online at many preserving websites.

Freezer Times	
Food	**Time**
Bacon and sausage	1–2 months
Banana (peeled and dipped in lemon juice)	4–6 months
Bread, pastries, and cakes	3 months
Butter	1 year
Casseroles	2–3 months
Cheese, aged/hard	6–8 months
Cherries, grapes, melons, and berries	8–12 months
Cookies (baked)	up to 1 year
Egg whites (removed from shell)	1 year
Fish, cooked	4–6 months
Fish, fatty fillet	2–3 months
Fish, lean fillet	4–6 months
Frozen dinners	3 months
Gravy	2 months
Ham	6 weeks
Hot dogs	6 weeks
Leftovers of spaghetti, chili, rice, beans, etc.	about 4 months
Lunch meat	6 weeks

Meat, cooked	3 months
Meat, ground raw	3 months
Meat, whole raw	4–12 months
Poultry, cooked	4 months
Poultry, cut raw	9 months
Poultry, whole raw	1 year
Shrimp	6–12 months
Soups	2–3 months
Tofu	5 months
Vegetables	8–12 months
Wild game, raw	8–12 months

Defrosting

As you start freezing your food in bulk, you may have questions about how to safely defrost food. The first rule of defrosting is not to leave anything at room temperature for hours at a time. Instead, there are three tried-and-true ways to safely defrost your food.

- **Leave the food in your refrigerator.** This takes a while, and it's wise to put some paper towels down or a platter underneath the item to catch any water or juices that run out during defrosting.

- **Put the food in a cold-water bath.** Keep the item in the wrapper or container, and if need be put it in an additional resealable bag for protection. It's recommended that you refresh the water every 30 minutes until the item is defrosted.

- **Use the defrost setting on your microwave.** Microwave wattage varies greatly from machine to machine, so watch carefully to make sure your food isn't being partially cooked, because that can give your food a rubbery texture. Again, you will want a plate or platter to catch any liquid that's released during the process for faster cleanup.

Of these three options, using the refrigerator is the recommended approach for the most sustainable results, because it protects the overall quality of the food and gives as similar a result to the fresh version as possible. Note that 1 pound of food takes about a day to defrost this way, so plan accordingly.

Preservation Pointers

Tea lovers will tell you that they never freeze tea leaves. The moisture in a freezer damages the leaves, and aromas can cause the scent of the tea to change. Instead, keep your tea in a sealed container in a dark area.

Refreezing

The beauty of thawing food in your refrigerator is that you can refreeze it quite safely, simply using what you need when you need it, and replacing what you don't in your stockpile. Just make sure the materials are kept properly cold during the time they're out of the freezer. You may lose a little moisture with meat and bread products, texture with vegetables, and flavor with juices, but there's no issue with microbial growth, because the average refrigerator keeps food at 30°F–48°F (30°F–40°F is ideal). Similarly, if you cook an item that was previously frozen, you can freeze any leftovers safely. Note, however, that some experts feel it's a good precaution to cook completely thawed meat before refreezing.

Preservation Pointers

What happens if your power goes out? If you leave your freezer closed, and it is in a cool part of the house (like your basement), food stays frozen up to 4 days in a well-stocked freezer. When the freezer is half-full or less, food will start to thaw in 24 hours.

Partially defrosted food is a little different. If there are still ice crystals in the package and the food has not been left at room temperature, it's relatively safe—just make sure there's no discoloration or odd odor. Any food that's been completely thawed to warm or room temperature should not be refrozen, and it should be discarded if it's been out longer than 2 hours.

Choosing a Freezer

While stocking for self-sustainability, there are many advantages to having an extra freezer. When stores have sales, you can buy in bulk and extend your grocery savings over several months. For whatever reason you are practicing self-sustainability, you could preserve an entire stockpile of frozen food to last you through any circumstance. Using your stockpile of bulk groceries, you can choose to prepare several meals in a marathon cooking session, and fill your freezer. This will give you the peace of mind of self-sustainability, and it will at the very least save you time in the months ahead for when you just don't feel like standing over the stove. Another advantage is that you'll always have extra food when family or friends stop over unexpectedly. With all that in mind, how do you choose a good freezer?

Cost Factors

This isn't going to be a minor purchase, but keep in mind that you are investing in self-sustainability. While you can get good comparative prices on basic freezers, there are a lot of other things to consider, including energy use, internal space, the product's warranty, and special features such as a quick-freeze cycle. Don't rush your choice. Most freezers will last ten to twelve years, so think about your future self-sustainability needs as well as your present ones.

Location and Space

Consider your space constraints. Where are you going to put the freezer? Does that space have a suitable electrical outlet? Always verify the power requirements with the manufacturer. Many new appliances require a 115-volt, three-pronged grounded power supply to run effectively. Placing the freezer in a cooler area of your home will help keep the cost of operating your freezer down, and it will help keep your food fresh for longer if the power goes out. Once you've found a spot, measure it. That measurement will indicate whether you need an upright or chest cooler. Bear in mind that upright freezers usually have many more features.

Upright or Chest Freezer

An upright freezer is very easy to access, especially if someone in your family has back problems. When you open the door, a fast visual survey will tell you what's inside. Uprights also typically offer conveniences like auto defrost and ice makers. Chest freezers, by comparison, have a larger capacity. They allow you to store oddly shaped items inside, and the internal temperature varies less than an upright. On the downside, you may forget what's at the bottom, and you'll have to manually defrost the freezer. While you're looking at features, see if there's a defrosting hose. This makes cleaning and upkeep much easier.

How Big?

By now you're probably starting to narrow your choices; don't forget to consider the size of the appliance. You know the space you've got, but that doesn't mean you have to buy a freezer that will fill that entire space. Most people get a larger freezer than they need, and unfortunately, that means a loss of energy. Consider how much food you'll be preserving and how long you want to create a sustainable stockpile for you and your family; then buy a freezer based on that volume.

Preservation Pointers

Frost-free freezers save people time, but they dry out foods more quickly. Without that feature, you must regularly thaw and clean your freezer and circulate stock. While you do so, make an inventory, including the date each item was frozen. Keep that list so you can regulate what you're stocking up on and make changes accordingly when you go shopping.

Energy Savings

Besides the size, check out the bright yellow EnergyGuide tag. The lower the number on that tag, the better. This is like looking at the miles per gallon a car gets. You want to save money with your freezer, not spend it all on electricity. Note that frost-free freezers use more energy than regular ones, and upright freezers are less energy efficient than chest coolers. Choosing where and how to save money when preserving will help you and your family be more self-sufficient in the long run.

CHAPTER FOUR

Drying

Drying was one of the first preserving methods ever used, probably because of its simplicity. And though it's much less commonplace these days, and most people get their dried foods pre-packaged from the store, drying is a great way to create a self-sustainable food stock. The long shelf life of dried food is a huge opportunity to be self-sustainable, because there isn't a lot of pressure to use and replace your dried foods. Without water content, food doesn't spoil, and it packs very neatly onto cupboard shelves. You can choose to save your dried foods for an emergency, or use them at your leisure and just as easily replace them in your stockpile. Although you can get commercial equipment designed for drying, there are items in your home right now that will fit the bill nicely. This chapter will explain the various types of dry preserving for self-sustainability and what foods they're best suited for.

Drying Methods

Drying is a little more alchemical than canning because of all the things that affect it. For example, temperature variations and humidity will both affect the drying process, specifically how long it will take. Pay attention to these things so that you can adjust your drying method accordingly. There are a variety of different ways to dry food, and you'll want a diverse range of dried foods for your pantry.

Preservation Pointers

When considering which drying method is best for you, don't forget to look at your environment. To sun dry food, for example, you'll need about 5 days of low humidity and high temperatures (95°F being ideal). While someone in Arizona might use this method with no difficulty, it's not likely to be practical for, say, someone in New York in January.

Air

Herbs and flowers are the most common air-dried foods. If you want to go the extra step in your self-sustainability and grow your own, harvest your herbs and flowers before 10:00 a.m. to retain the greatest amount of essential oil for aroma and flavor. As the day grows later, the heat of the sun causes the oils to retreat into the plant stem or dry up altogether. If you're hanging the plants, don't bundle too many together; about six stems is good. Hang them upside down from a string in a dry, warm spot with a paper lunch bag draped loosely over the bundle to keep it free from dust and to protect the bundle against sunlight. Use a toothpick to make holes in the bag to allow air to circulate. The plant matter should be dry and ready to add to your stockpile in 14 days.

An alternative method of drying is to remove the flower petals or herb leaves from the stem and lay them on a screen. It's very impor-

tant that the screening material be clean and that the plant pieces don't touch each other. Place a piece of cheesecloth (or a large paper bag with pinholes in it) over the top of the screens. Again, this protects the flowers and herbs from airborne dust and dirt. Keep the trays out of the sunlight and in a cool, dry area. As with hanging, it will take about 2 weeks to thoroughly dry the plant matter.

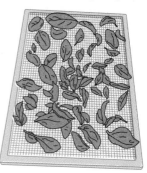

Sun Drying

While it may seem like the most efficient and easiest method of drying food, sun drying for sustainability is not always practicable due to geography. You need several days of 90°F–100°F temperatures and low humidity for successful, even preserving. Additionally, great caution is required to keep the items safe from bugs, dirt, wandering animals, and other hazards. Sun drying is not recommended in areas with high levels of air pollution.

Preservation Pointers

A wide variety of food can be dried and kept for long periods of time, including fish, fruit, edible flowers, meat, vegetables, and herbs. The taste and texture of dried food is different than fresh or frozen, so make small batches at first to get used to the process and the tastes. Keep a list of items that you and your family like best, so you know which items to stock in bulk.

If you live in a region with consistent hot, dry weather, you can look into commercial sun dryers that use screening to protect the foods. If the weather changes unexpectedly, it's best to bring the items inside and finish the drying using your oven.

Pressing

Pressing as a preserving method is most commonly seen with flowers. While some people use pressed flowers and herb parts for decoration, many are edible and are a great source of nutrients, especially vitamins A and C. Flowers that are edible include angelica, apple blossom, borage, carnation, chrysanthemum, dandelion, jasmine, lavender, lilac, marigold, nasturtium, rose, squash flowers, and many more. They can be stored with your other dried foods as long as the flowers were grown organically. Flowers, like herbs, should be gathered early in the morning as soon as they're open a bit. This makes cleaning them off easier. Gently run the flowers under cool water to remove any debris. Leave the plant parts on a paper towel while you set up your pressing method. Your layering materials include several pieces of 8" × 11" cardboard, some newspaper, paper towels, and a heavy 8" × 11" book.

Begin by putting the cardboard on a flat surface. On top of that, put three sheets of newspaper, followed by three sheets of paper towels. Lay the flowers or herbs on the top sheet, leaving space between them. Over the top of this, place three more paper towels, three more sheets of newspaper, and another piece of cardboard. You can keep going for two or three more layers, topping everything with the heavy book; good-sized stones or bricks also work very well. Your plant matter will press dry in about a month, so you may want to have several labeled plant-drying projects going at once, depending on your stockpiling needs.

Microwave Drying

Microwave ovens vary in their overall power, which makes providing tried-and-true instructions for their use difficult. Overall, herbs are the items best suited to this preservation method, but you have to be careful to not under-dry or burn your herbs.

Take some fresh herb leaves or flowers and put them on a paper plate. Dry the herbs at 50 percent power in 30-second intervals. Each time you check the herbs, turn them over. If your microwave platform doesn't rotate, you'll also need to rotate the herbs on the plate. Most herbs dry in

2 minutes using this method, but they may not be well suited for stock-piling in bulk, because the microwave evaporates many oils that make herbs flavorful and aromatic.

Oven Drying

While using the microwave makes things faster, using your conventional oven for drying may be costly. Because you're leaving food on low heat for many hours, the bottom line on your electric or gas bill may price this method right out of your comfort zone.

On the other hand, oven drying is very simple, and lends well to drying items that you can store in bulk for very long periods of time. Consider the pros and cons of each drying technique as you adopt a self-sustainable drying method that works best for you and your family. Preheat your oven to 140°F, and prep your food according to the recipe instructions. Use large baking sheets to dry the food. Most baking sheets hold up to 2 pounds of food. Unless you have a very large oven, it's suggested that you dry no more than three trays at a time, shifting their positions and turning the food every 30 minutes for the best results. To maximize on heat and energy, try to keep the door of the oven open about 2" throughout this time. You'll have more even results, as this conservative circulation method improves airflow and decreases the amount of heat lost when you need to circulate the drying items.

Preservation Pointers

If you have any stainless-steel screens, put these on your oven racks to elevate the food. This will give all sides of the items more air exposure and improve even drying. Aluminum screens are not recommended for this purpose because they can impart an odd flavor.

Food Dehydrator

If you think you'll be stocking up on lots of dry food for self-sustainability, you may want to consider buying a food dehydrator. Using a commercial electric dehydrator takes half the time as drying in an oven, making it perfect for the energy-conscious consumer. An additional benefit is that these devices are created specifically to maintain air circulation, sustain even heating, and safeguard nutritional value. Fruits, herbs, and meats are good candidates for the dehydrator.

Circular Food Dehydrator

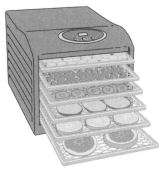

Square Food Dehydrator

The market for dehydrators has grown, which means you can find some great optional features—for a price. You can pay more than $300 for a stainless-steel dehumidifier with 16 cubic feet of interior space, but most self-sufficient home preservers don't need anything quite so impressive. If you plan to spend between $60 and $75, you'll usually get a good-quality machine.

Look for machine features that will make self-sustainable drying easier. For example, a temperature gauge lets you adjust the heat to specific food groups, allowing you to produce a higher quality dried item. Additionally, you want a dehydrator that fits in your kitchen comfortably and has enough trays to make several layers of dried goods, a timer to keep things from overcooking, and a good warranty. Last but not least, dishwasher-safe parts save you a lot of time.

For Drying Success: Freshness, Attentiveness, and Airflow

Like most food-preservation methods for self-sustainability, when drying, "fresh is best" is your mantra. The sooner you begin drying items after they've been harvested, the happier you'll be with the results. This will maximize the nutrition in your dried foods, ensuring that your dried food stockpile for your family is as healthy as possible.

With self-sustainable drying, it may be one of the few times in cooking when you'll hear "faster is better." When you carefully and quickly dry goods, it helps create a continuity of texture and ensures that the center of the item doesn't retain moisture. Nonetheless, most drying techniques do take a little while, so allow for the time in your schedule. If you have to stop in the middle of drying something, you're opening the door for microbial growth. Set aside certain weekends for drying in bulk so that you can create a large store of healthy dried foods for you and your family.

You don't have to over-monitor the drying process if you're following the temperature and time guidelines provided for the chosen method. It's suggested, however, that you keep an eye on the food in the last hour. You don't want to burn your efforts, and due diligence during the last hour helps you avoid that. While you may want to dry different types of food in the same appliance at once in order to maximize your output for your stockpile, it must be done carefully, because fruits, vegetables, and even meats can contain very different amounts of liquid.

Drying doesn't require a lot of fancy equipment, but some items come in handy if you're going to be drying in bulk for self-sustainability. A countertop scale helps you measure out portions for recipes, and a range thermometer allows you to adjust the temperature for even drying in the oven. If money is tight, put these on the wish list for another day.

Finally—and this cannot be stressed enough—good air circulation is your best ally in successfully drying products, no matter what process you're using. To get the best benefit from that circulation, remember to rotate and stir the drying items periodically. This ensures you'll have the most sustainable product because it exposes each side to the air to ensure even drying.

Drying Fruit

Bargains are great, but you don't want items that are overripe or damaged for your dried food pantry. Pick out a piece of fruit that you'd put out that day for someone to enjoy. When you get the fruit home, the sooner you can begin the drying process, the better. If something deters you, store the fruit in a cool area until you can prepare it for your chosen drying method.

Cleaning and Slicing

All fruit requires a good washing before you begin. With items like peaches or apples, you'll need to get rid of the inedible core or pit. Peel the fruit before slicing it thinly. If you're drying something like grapes, treat the skins to a swim in boiling water, use a strainer to dunk them in a bowl of cold water, then lay them aside to dry. This method is called cracking, and it lets air into the fruit for better sustainable drying.

Preservation Pointers

Sulfuring preserves fruits' colors for the longest amount of time and helps them retain vitamins A and C. By comparison, ascorbic acid is about half as effective, and lemon juice is a third as effective. However, some people have sulfur allergies, which makes lemon juice or ascorbic acid appealing.

Battling Browning

Once sliced, fruit begins to brown fairly quickly. For the most sustainable product, you want to keep the browning to a minimum because it does impact the overall quality of dried fruit. If you'll be drying large amounts of fruit, you may want to buy ascorbic acid, a popular ingredient for offsetting oxidation. Just add the ascorbic acid to the fruit once it's cut (1 teaspoon dissolved in 1 cup of water for 5 quarts of soft fruit like peaches; 2 teaspoons for hard fruit like apples).

If the results obtained by ascorbic acid aren't as sustainable as you would like, try a solution of sulfite instead. You need 1 tablespoon of food-grade sodium bisulfite (available in drugstores) in $\frac{1}{2}$ gallon water. Soak the fruit for about 7 minutes; leave light-colored fruit in for a full 10 minutes. Afterward, drain and dry. Soaking lengthens the drying process, so factor in extra time.

Budget about 6–12 hours to completely dry fruit pieces. Smaller slices or pieces dry the fastest, so you may want to dry your fruit stockpile in very small pieces for the most efficient and sustainable results. Always cut open a piece and check the interior to make sure the process is complete.

Drying Vegetables

Not all vegetables take well to drying. When you start thinking about drying vegetables, consider which ones have the shortest shelf life and which of those might be better suited to freezing. For example, the texture of asparagus doesn't hold up well with drying and dehydration, so as you become more self-sustainable, you may decide that this is one vegetable you'll freeze instead.

Your vegetables should be fully grown and in peak condition. If you can harvest them from your garden, that's fantastic. However, only buy or harvest the vegetables that you know you'll be drying and stockpiling that day. This keeps your kitchen space more manageable and will help you organize your pantry as you add more dried foods. Thoroughly clean and cut the vegetables to the desired size, remembering that the larger the piece, the longer the drying time. Most vegetables require a fast blanching to stop enzymes from continuing to break down the plant matter. The exceptions to this rule include okra, onions, carrots, mushrooms, and peppers.

Preservation Pointers

When a drying recipe calls for you to blanch a vegetable, don't throw that water away! It's rich in flavor and vitamins. Instead, reduce it down over a low flame, adding whatever spices you like, and freeze it for future soups, gravies, and stews.

Some vegetable parts, such as celery leaf, dry quickly; other parts will take as long as comparable fruit pieces. Dried vegetables are hard and crunchy. As you build your self-sufficient pantry, keep each type of dried vegetable separately in airtight, carefully labeled containers. Keep them away from sunlight or heat for the greatest longevity.

Drying Herbs

There's an old saying among herbalists: Don't grow mint unless you want a lot of it. As someone who is working toward self-sufficiency, this may be exactly what you want! Members of the mint family have a reputation for being overly hearty, which also makes them an excellent candidate for drying, since you'll have an abundance to stock. And mint is only one of the many herbs you can dry. In ancient times, dried herbs were commonly sold along trade routes, and merchants used legends about their healing powers to boost prices. Drying was the easiest way to retain flavor, a necessity when traveling through different environmental conditions. For modern self-sustainable preservers, drying is an efficient way to get organic spices in a relatively short time frame.

Choosing and Cleaning Herbs

The self-sustainable "fresher is better" mantra also applies to herbs. When growing herbs at home, new growth bears better flavors than larger, older parts. It's also a sustainable idea to harvest these early in the morning to conserve as much natural oil as possible. Once you've purchased or harvested the plants, make sure there are no dark leaves or any pieces that look withered. Remove those pieces along with the stalk. Put the herbs in a colander to rinse and drip dry. The herbs are now ready to be dried using whatever method you prefer.

Preservation Pointers

If there's little or no aroma when you open a container of dried herbs, that means the plant has lost its remaining aromatic oils, which also give the herb flavor. Toss the dried herb into your compost heap; it's no longer useful for cooking.

Timing Is Everything

As you become more comfortable with self-sustainable drying processes, you'll become more familiar with the exact timing of drying different items. In general, drying will take an average of 3 hours. In the microwave, sandwich the herbs between pieces of paper towels and use a low setting for 30-second intervals until the herbs are crunchy dry. Store the herbs in airtight containers in your pantry. Label and place them in a cool, dark area of the pantry. In this form, herbs have a shelf life of one year for the best results.

Drying Meat, Poultry, and Fish

Drying is one of the oldest, most traditional, and most sustainable forms of preserving meat. Not only can dried meat last you and your family a long time, it travels well and doesn't weigh as much once it's dehydrated. Many people associate dried meat with meat jerky. Making jerky at home is self-sufficient and cost effective. A pound of turkey jerky, for example, can cost upward of $6, depending on where you live. A pound of ground turkey and jerky spices costs about $2.50. Even after running a dehydrator, you're still saving money, and you know exactly what's in your snack!

Preparation Process

When preparing your own meat and fish for drying, choose very lean cuts of meat or fish, and immediately get rid of excess fat, which can go rancid even after drying. Cutting with the grain, slice the meat into ⅛"-thick pieces about 1" wide. You'll want a good, sharp knife. Dry the meat as it is or add salt, pepper, or other spices as desired. Cover the meat and let it sit in the refrigerator for 8–12 hours before drying it for the most sustainable results.

Preservation Pointers

Freeze your meat halfway so that cutting it is a piece of cake! If you're drying game meat, freezing it completely for several weeks will kill parasites. When you're ready to dry it, defrost it only partially for cutting.

Dry Aging

Dry aging beef for self-sustainability can be done at home if you're exceedingly careful. Always begin with USDA Prime or Choice cuts from a trusted butcher. Rinse and dry the roast, then cover it with three sheets of cheesecloth or with an absolutely clean, new cotton towel. You can also rest the roast on a rack inside a plastic food container that you've poked full of holes to allow air in. Place the wrapped or sealed roast on a rack in the lowest part of your refrigerator.

Dry-aging experts usually age meat for 10–21 days. However, while taking on sustainable home preserving, your safest bet is aging the meat for 3–7 days. On each of those days, you will need to replace the cheesecloth or towel with a fresh one. Make sure there is nothing in your refrigerator with a strong aroma, and make sure nothing can leak onto your roast. After 7 days, the roast will shrink about 8–10 percent and gain a distinctively rich flavor. It's essential to get an accurate thermometer for your refrigerator when dry aging beef. In order to keep the meat safe from spoiling, the temperature inside the refrigerator should remain consistently below 35°F. If you're going to be stockpiling dry-aged beef, you may want to dry all your beef cuts at once to make the most of your refrigeration space at a time.

Finally, unwrap the roast, carefully cutting off any exterior dried meat or fat. Cook this as it is or slice it into steaks. This meat may be frozen for future use. It has a shelf life of about 4 months.

CHAPTER FIVE

Pickling

People across the globe have been pickling foods for self-sustainability for thousands of years. It was among the most popular preserving methods for sailors, both because it was safe and because folks genuinely liked the flavors pickling produces. These days, while it's easy to get pickles at the store, it's hard to find the varieties that you and your family enjoy, and it's even harder to find healthy options for pickles due to the high volume of sodium added to mass-produced grocery store pickles. Making your own pickles gives you the freedom to save and store delicious food for you and your family while knowing exactly what ingredients are going into your pickle jars. Even those who are just pickling as a hobby are creating a small self-sufficient stock by preserving food on their own. In this chapter, you'll learn about the different types of pickles, the equipment you'll need, how exactly to make brine, and how to make the healthiest and most sustainable pickles for you and your family.

Pickling 101

At a basic level, pickling preserves food in brine consisting of salt and water (1½ tablespoons salt to 1 quart water), vinegar and water (1:3 ratio), sugar and water (1 cup salt and sugar per gallon), and additional spices to create distinctive tastes.

There are four basic types of pickles. The first is fresh pack, which is like the refrigerator pickles covered later in this chapter. From a sustainability standpoint, they are very simple to prepare. The second are fruit pickles, which are prepared with a sugar-vinegar syrup. Chutneys and relishes are a third type of pickle; you'll find recipes for those in Chapter 6. Finally, the most popular are salt-cured or brined pickles. No matter what type of pickle you'll be stocking, always start with firm fruits or vegetables, fresh spices, and clean water. When harvesting your own fruits and vegetables, do so early in the morning and refrigerate them immediately before preparing all your pickling equipment for the most sustainable results. This is also true of store-bought items. Heat makes pickled items softer.

Basic Equipment

One of the great beauties of pickling for self-sustainability is that it doesn't require a lot of fancy equipment. Stainless steel and glass are ideal for pickling projects. Aluminum, enamel, and iron pots or tools aren't recommended because of brine's natural acidity; when the acid reacts with those bases, it changes the flavor of the resulting food items. The following list includes some of the items you'll want for pickling:

- Stone jar or crockery for fermenting (Note: You will need a plate or other cover that fits inside your fermenting jar. This holds the pickles beneath the brine. Kitchen plates work well.)
- Paring knife
- Vegetable peeler
- Ladle
- Funnel
- Measuring tools

- Large bowl, plastic zip-top bag, or plastic food container (these may substitute for the stone jar or crockery as a fermenting vessel)

- Pots large enough for simmering the brine and spices

- Water-bath canner (if you're planning to put up the pickles)

- Storage jars or containers

Fermenting Jar

Embracing Brine

Brining has become a very popular method in self-sustainability pickling, but it's also useful as a marinade. For example, some people who prepare deep-fried turkey swear by herb-laced brine as one method for making a truly flavorful bird. The longer an item remains in brine, the more the base changes the taste and texture of the food, so keep this in mind as you create different pickles while stocking your pantry.

Brining is very easy and very popular for meat because the salt helps keep it moist during the cooking process. To the foundation of salt and water, many cooks now add other spices to infuse every part of the meat with flavor (rather than flavoring just the exterior, as sometimes happens with a marinade). Meats that benefit from brining include lean poultry, pork, and seafood.

When preparing meat in brine for sustainability, it's very important to soak it in the refrigerator at about 40°F. Before the meat goes in, both the brine and meat should already be at the correct temperature. This prevents bacterial growth. Smaller cuts of meat, which may be easier for you to stockpile in bulk, accept brine within about 4 hours. Note that brined meat cooks in about two-thirds of the time of unbrined meat. The same concept holds true for vegetables, fruits, and flowers. Whatever spices you add to fermenting or pickling brine are transported with the salt into the food.

Salt by Any Name

Table salt and sea salt are the most common ones used in brining. While some folks like a gourmet touch like fleur de sel and Hawaiian salt, they're oftentimes too costly for efficient and sustainable preserving. Recipes will usually specify a variety of salt. If you're going to substitute, 1 cup table salt is equal to 1 ½ cups kosher salt.

Brine Containers

As you buy containers, make sure they are able to store easily in your pantry alongside your other stockpiles of preserved food. Food-storage containers, large cooking bowls, and stainless-steel stockpots all work very well as brine receptacles. Alternatively, if you're stockpiling your pickles and need to make a large quantity of brine, try a clean cooler (this

needs to be sterilized). Remember that you'll need enough brine to completely cover the food. If you can't guess, put the food in the container and cover it with plain water. Measure that water and add your salt accordingly. Note that while you want to be as efficient and sustainable as possible with your ingredients and materials, you should never reuse brine.

Hotter...Colder...Hotter

As you become more familiar with different meats and brines, you may want to adjust your meat brine according to the temperature at which you plan to cook it. When stockpiling, know that slow- and low-cooked meat receives more sugar and salt compared to high-heat (grilling or broiling) meat. Generally, the slow-cooked brine takes ¼ cup kosher salt and sugar to 1 pint of water. For high-heat cooking, use 1 quart water, 1 tablespoon sugar, and 2 tablespoons kosher salt. In terms of brining time, about 1 hour per pound is a good measure. Make sure to allow enough time if you'll be brining in bulk to create a bigger pickle stockpile.

Pickle Brining

Pickle brine includes vinegar for curing along with the traditional salt and/or sugar. Cucumbers are far and away the most popular vegetable for pickling. They are also a great starter vegetable for pickling before you move into different items and diversify your pickle stock. They are best purchased or harvested unwaxed, when they're small and very firm. Brining waxed cucumbers won't work because the salt cannot penetrate the skin. The basic brine for pickling is 1 quart water to $\frac{1}{2}$ cup salt. It's important that the vegetables remain submerged in the brine throughout the fermenting period. It takes about a month for a whole pickle to be completely fermented. The best test is to cut one open and look for uniform color.

Preservation Pointers

Always use the amount of vinegar or salt suggested in a recipe. If you find the blend is too harsh for you, add a pinch of sugar to balance out the tartness. Both vinegar and salt are important to safeguard against bacterial growth.

Now you can rinse the pickle mixture and move the vegetable into a mixture of 3 parts good-quality vinegar (5 percent acidity) with 1 part filtered water and any additional flavorings. Cider and malt vinegar are mild and work well in sweet pickle recipes, while white vinegar is the most commonly used because it doesn't discolor the vegetables. You can certainly substitute one type of vinegar for another in your recipes, as long as the vinegar has the 5 percent acidity necessary for pickling.

If a recipe calls for sugar, you could try substituting honey if white sugar isn't in your diet. Use about $\frac{3}{4}$ cup honey for every 1 cup of sugar. Be aware this changes the flavor of the end product. At this juncture, you can store the pickles in the refrigerator for snacking, or can them and stock up your pantry. However, pickles fermented in this way will lose some crispness in the canning process.

Refrigerator Pickling

Refrigerator pickling (also known as quick pickling) is fast and easy, and you can use it to pickle any vegetable or fruit. It can come in handy while creating quick stores of pickles for you and your family to be eaten in a relatively short amount of time. Quick pickling won't preserve your food nearly as long as other preserving processes, but it's tasty and can save you time. The following directions explain how to pickle cucumbers, which are among the most popular vegetables for refrigerator pickling because they take exceedingly well to the process. Other good options include cauliflower, baby onions, and sliced carrots.

1. Find the freshest, crispest produce that has no signs of being past its prime. You'll need about 6 (approximately 4" long) cucumbers for a quart jar. Carefully wash the cucumbers and slice them into bite-sized pieces.

2. Sterilize your jars. If you have a sterilizing cycle on your dishwasher, you can prepare the jars while you're cutting! Otherwise, fill a large stockpot with water, add your jars and lids, and bring them to a full boil.

3. Mix together and heat 6 cups water, 2 cups white vinegar, $\frac{1}{2}$ cup sugar (if you want sweet pickles), $\frac{1}{2}$ cup canning and pickling salt, and 1 teaspoon each of your desired spices to a simmer. Dill and garlic are both great flavors, as are sliced onion, mustard seeds, and celery seeds. You may also want to add $\frac{1}{2}$ teaspoon alum for crispness.

4. While the brine heats, pack the cucumbers into the sterilized jars, leaving about $\frac{1}{4}$" headspace at the top.

5. Pour the hot brine over the cucumbers; cover. Let sit at room temperature for 24 hours. Chill and enjoy.

Pickling Olives

Historically, olives and olive oil were important items throughout Asia Minor, where they have been cultivated and used for self-sustainability for thousands of years. Olives are long-lived evergreens that can reach a height of more than twenty feet and begin to yield fruit by the time they are about five years of age. The fruit of the trees has many uses, but they cannot be consumed raw. They have to be brined or otherwise processed, meaning that the idea of pickled olives is really a twice-pickling method.

For success in pickling and stockpiling olives, select ones that are firm, and don't attempt to mix different types of olives together. Since you'll probably get olives that have already been brined once, it's acceptable and even preferable to mix one type of olives with garlic, onions, or other items for pickling as you create a diverse range of pickled items for your pantry. To keep the olives as firm as possible, do not cook them in brine. Instead, mix them with other chosen ingredients and pour the brine over the top. In this form, the pickled olive mix can be refrigerated or canned but not frozen. The pickled olives last about 3 months in the refrigerator; canned olives should be used in 1 year. Next you'll learn how to handle any pickling problems that may come up as you build up your pickle stockpile.

Troubleshooting Pickling Problems

What's a cook to do when the pickles turn out less than perfect? This list includes common problems and their solutions.

- Bitter pickles indicate too much vinegar; check the recipe. Note: This can also be caused by using salt substitutes.

- Cloudy pickles are a warning that your pickles may have spoiled—especially if they were fresh packed. The introduction of an airborne yeast, the use of metal pans, adding table salt, and using hard water during production can also have this effect. If the pickled item seems greasy or smells funny, throw it out.

- Discolored pickles are usually the fault of the pan or hard water, but strong spices can also bleed into pickles, giving them a different hue.

- Green- or blue-tinted garlic isn't cause for concern. It just means that the garlic absorbed the metals in your cooking utensils or the garlic you used was young. It's still perfectly safe to eat.

- Hollow cucumbers are safe to eat. The cucumber may have been too big or may have been hollow when canning. If a cucumber floats in water, it's not a good pickling cucumber. The brine may also have been too weak or too strong.

- Pale coloring may mean your produce was exposed to light or was of poor quality.

- Dark coloring may result from minerals in the water, the use of different vinegar (like malt vinegar), overcooking, or the use of iodized salt in processing. If you didn't change any components, darkening may indicate spoilage. When in doubt, throw it out!

- Bubbly brine is a sign that your food has begun to spoil. Throw these pickles out.

- Pink pickles may result if you use overly ripe dill in your pickle blend. The introduction of yeast is another possible reason. If the pickles are soft, the liquid cloudy, or the food feels slimy, it's likely a yeast problem, and the pickles should be discarded.

- Slimy pickles can result from a variety of issues. The amount of salt or vinegar used in the mix may not have been sufficient, the pickles may not have been totally covered by brine, the canning process may not have been followed correctly, yeast may have been introduced, moldy spices may have been used, jars may have been improperly sealed, or the pickles may have been kept in too hot an area (70°F is the best temperature to encourage proper pickling). These are not safe to eat.

- Bland pickles may result from use of cucumbers that were not meant for pickling. Store-bought cucumbers often have a waxy coating. The brine can't penetrate this coating, and the resulting pickles are less flavorful. If you must use this type of cucumber, slice and salt it for about 1 hour, then rinse and pickle. This will open the pores, letting the brine in.

- Shriveled pickles may mean the vinegar is too strong, the salt concentration too high, or the pickles overprocessed. Measure carefully and watch the clock!

- Mixed flavors usually mean the size of the vegetables wasn't even. The larger the cut, the more time a vegetable takes to accept flavor.

- Mushy pickles can result from using the wrong type of cucumber or overprocessing. If you have a choice of what to buy or grow, look for lemon cucumbers as well as little leaf, Saladin, and Edmonson varieties. You can use food-grade alum or grape leaves in the bottom of the jar to improve crispness.

- Mold or dirt on a jar often indicates it wasn't properly sealed; some of the brine has gotten out onto the rim, meaning that bacteria can also get into the jar. Don't eat these.

Whenever you're confronted with a jar you don't feel quite right about, it's best to err on the side of caution and throw it out.

CHAPTER SIX

Condiments

Garlic Honey Mustard

This Garlic Honey Mustard is much more natural, healthy, and sustainable than the store-bought version. Use this zesty condiment on pork, chicken, or your next hoagie.

Sustainable Storage: Lasts up to 6 months.

Makes: 2 cups

Ingredients

¼ cup freshly ground yellow mustard seeds

½ cup honey

¼ cup whole dark mustard seeds

½ cup malt or white vinegar

1 tablespoon yellow mustard powder

1 tablespoon finely minced garlic

⅛ teaspoon salt

⅛ teaspoon freshly ground black pepper

1. Thoroughly mix all ingredients in a small bowl. Taste and adjust seasonings for personal preferences.

2. To make the mustard thinner, add more vinegar; to make it thicker, add more mustard powder or honey.

3. Pack into sterilized jars, leaving at least ¼" headspace at the top of each jar. Make sure to remove all air bubbles. Wipe rims and place sterilized lid on each jar. Tightly screw on sterilized screw bands, and process in a water-bath canner for 15 minutes.

4. Move jars to a cooling surface, leaving plenty of space between the jars. Check all the lids when cool, tightening as needed. If any of the jars did not seal, refrigerate or freeze instead.

Onion Bourbon Mustard

This recipe's ingredients are most likely already in your house, so no extra shopping is needed. This is a great starter recipe for working toward self-sustainability.

Sustainable Storage:
Lasts up to 1 month in the refrigerator or up to 6 months in the freezer.

Makes: 2 cups

Ingredients

$^1\!/_4$ cup diced onion

1 tablespoon extra-virgin olive oil

$^1\!/_2$ teaspoon granulated sugar

$^1\!/_2$ cup honey

$^1\!/_2$ cup firmly packed dark brown sugar

$^1\!/_2$ cup apple cider vinegar

4 tablespoons mustard powder

2 tablespoons whole yellow mustard seeds

2 tablespoons freshly ground yellow mustard seeds

2 tablespoons freshly ground horseradish

$^1\!/_2$ cup bourbon whiskey

$^1\!/_8$ teaspoon salt

$^1\!/_8$ teaspoon freshly ground black pepper

1. In a small skillet over medium heat, sauté onion in olive oil. As it begins to brown, sprinkle it with granulated sugar to caramelize.

2. Mix onion, honey, brown sugar, vinegar, mustard powder, whole mustard seeds, ground mustard seeds, horseradish, and whiskey in a blender on low speed until well incorporated.

3. Pour the resulting mixture into a medium saucepan.

4. Heat mustard over low heat until it comes to a boil. Continue boiling until mustard reaches the desired consistency.

5. Cool and add salt and pepper to taste. If freezing, transfer into freezer-safe containers, leaving $^1\!/_4$" headspace for expansion.

Preservation Pointers

There are two common types of mustard seed, brown and yellow. The good news for home preservers is that mustard grows easily up to Zone 3. Wait until your weather is steadily above 55°F to sow seeds (1" apart, ¼" deep). You will need to thin the plants later. Come late summer, when the seed pods turn yellow, they're ready to harvest.

Heirloom Mustard Pickles

These are the kinds of pickles often seen on our grandparents' tables. While the spices may change a little, the self-sufficiency that these pickles inspire remains consistent. If alum doesn't agree with your stomach, use grape leaves at the bottom of the jar to achieve crispiness instead.

Sustainable Storage:
Lasts 1 year when canned or 6–8 months in the freezer.

Makes: 4 quarts

Ingredients

4 cups chopped (1" dice) onions

4 cups chopped (1" dice) cucumbers

4 cups chopped (1" dice) small green tomatoes

1 medium head cauliflower, trimmed and chopped into 1" dice

2 medium green bell peppers, seeded and chopped into 1" dice

1 gallon water

2 cups salt

$\frac{1}{8}$ teaspoon alum

4 cups granulated sugar

3 tablespoons celery seeds

$\frac{2}{3}$ cup yellow mustard

$4\frac{1}{4}$ cups white vinegar

1. Put chopped vegetables into a large bowl; cover with water, salt, and alum.

2. Put a plate over top of vegetables so they stay below brine; leave at room temperature 24 hours.

3. The next day, in a large pot over medium heat, warm vegetables and brine mixture to scalding; remove from heat and drain vegetables. If freezing, cool and transfer into freezer-safe containers, leaving $\frac{1}{4}$" headspace for expansion. If canning, immediately pack into sterilized jars.

4. Put remaining ingredients in a large pot over low heat. Simmer until thickened. Pour sauce evenly over pickles in freezer-safe containers or canning jars. If canning, make sure to remove all air bubbles from jars. Leave $\frac{1}{4}$" headspace at the top of each jar. Wipe rims and place sterilized lid on each jar. Tightly screw on sterilized screw bands, and process in a water-bath canner for 10 minutes.

5. Move the jars to a cooling surface, leaving plenty of space between the jars. Check all the lids when cool, tightening as needed. If any of the jars did not seal, refrigerate or freeze instead.

Burmese-Style Mustard Greens

Preserving greens ensures that you'll always have a healthy and sustainable source of vitamins at hand. Try it with Chinese five-spice powder in place of the ginger.

Sustainable Storage:
Lasts up to 1 year when canned or in the freezer.

Makes: 2 quarts

Ingredients

$1\frac{1}{2}$ pounds mustard greens, blanched for 30 seconds

3 cups thinly sliced carrots

$\frac{1}{2}$ pound shallots, peeled and diced

2 medium red chili peppers, seeded and diced

2 teaspoons salt

2 teaspoons firmly packed dark brown sugar

1 teaspoon grated fresh ginger

$\frac{1}{3}$ cup dark beer

$\frac{2}{3}$ cup malt vinegar

1. Soak blanched greens in hot water until wilted, then chop into $\frac{1}{4}$" slices.

2. Mix remaining ingredients in a large bowl; add the greens and turn to coat evenly.

3. Cover with a plate for weight; secure with plastic wrap. Let sit for 24 hours in refrigerator. Greens can be refrigerated, frozen, or canned. Flavor improves with aging.

4. If freezing, transfer greens to freezer-safe containers, leaving $\frac{1}{4}$" headspace for expansion. If canning, pack into sterilized jars, leaving 1" headspace at the top of each jar. Make sure to remove all air bubbles. Wipe rims and place sterilized lid on each jar. Tightly screw on sterilized screw bands, and process in a water-bath canner for 15 minutes.

5. Move jars to a cooling surface, leaving plenty of space between the jars. Check all the lids when cool, tightening as needed. If any of the jars did not seal, refrigerate or freeze instead.

Louisiana-Style Mustard

Having a few jars of this mustard in your freezer means you'll never need to rely on grocery stores again for a spicy mustard. This piquant mustard works as a braise for pork and chicken, not to mention a sizzling spread for your ham sandwich.

Sustainable Storage: Lasts up to 1 year in the freezer. Refrigerate after opening.

Makes: 2½ cups

Ingredients

1 cup whole yellow mustard seeds

1 cup dry white wine or champagne

1 medium clove garlic, peeled and minced

1 teaspoon celery seeds

1 teaspoon ground allspice

½ teaspoon salt

½ teaspoon Worcestershire sauce

½ teaspoon prepared hot sauce

2 tablespoons white vinegar

2 tablespoons malt vinegar

1. Heat a small skillet over medium heat and toss in mustard seeds. When the seeds begin to pop, remove the pan from heat and cover with a heavy, clean cloth until the seeds cool.

2. Coarsely grind toasted seeds using a rolling pin or mortar and pestle.

3. In a small saucepan, mix the wine, garlic, celery seeds, allspice, salt, Worcestershire, and hot sauce. Bring to a simmer over low heat, stirring regularly for 5 minutes.

4. While the wine mixture simmers, mix the ground mustard seeds in a small bowl with white vinegar and malt vinegar, stirring to make an even paste.

5. Bring the wine mixture to a full boil, then slowly add the mustard paste, stirring until all ingredients are well incorporated.

6. Pour the mustard into sterilized jars, leaving ¼" headspace. Cap.

7. Let sit overnight before transferring to freezer-safe containers, leaving ¼" headspace for expansion.

Green Tomato Relish

This is a great way to spread the sustainability of your garden throughout the year. Use this recipe to preserve your green garden tomatoes before they ripen. Serve with hot dogs, bratwursts, and anything else you like!

Sustainable Storage:
Lasts up to 1 year.

Makes: 12–15 quarts

Ingredients

20–25 pounds solid, hard, totally green tomatoes, cored and cut into bite-sized chunks

1 (4-pound) container pickling salt

10–12 pounds onions, peeled and sliced

4 large green bell peppers, seeded and sliced

4 large red bell peppers, seeded and sliced

4 large orange bell peppers, seeded and sliced

4 large yellow bell peppers, seeded and sliced

8 cups apple cider vinegar, divided

2–3 gallons white vinegar, divided

10 cups granulated sugar, divided

1/2 cup mixed pickling spice, divided

2–4 dried hot peppers, divided

8 dried bay leaves, divided

1. Layer enough tomatoes to cover the bottom of a very large stockpot. Sprinkle well with pickling salt, then repeat layers until all tomatoes are in the pot. Cover with a clean white cotton dishcloth. Let sit in a draft-free area for 2–4 hours. The pickling salt will draw moisture from the hard tomatoes. If it is a very warm day, 2 hours is sufficient to soften tomatoes a bit.

2. Rinse tomatoes in cold water at least twice. Drain. Divide between 2 large stockpots.

3. Divide onions and peppers equally between the stockpots.

4. Divide the cider vinegar and white vinegar between the stockpots to cover vegetables. Divide sugar evenly between stockpots. Stir well.

5. To make two spice balls, fold a square of cheesecloth twice and place 1/4 cup mixed pickling spice, half the dried hot peppers, and 4 bay leaves on the surface. Gather up the corners and tie with kitchen string. Repeat with remaining pickling spice, hot peppers, and bay leaves. Place one spice ball into each stockpot. Sink it down toward the middle.

Continued on next page

Green Tomato Relish cont.

6. Stir ingredients in each stockpot well. Cover and bring to a boil over high heat. Reduce heat and simmer for 30–45 minutes, until tomatoes are tender but not mushy.

7. Remove and discard spice balls.

8. Use a slotted spoon to pack vegetables into sterilized jars, packing down with a plastic knife to remove air bubbles.

9. Add hot brine to jars to cover vegetables, leaving 1" headspace. Wipe rims and place sterilized lid on each jar. Tightly screw on sterilized screw bands, and process in a water-bath canner for 20 minutes.

10. Move the jars to a cooling surface, leaving plenty of space between the jars. Check all the lids when cool, tightening as needed. If any of the jars did not seal, refrigerate or freeze instead.

Caramelized Red Onion Relish

You and your family will enjoy this sustainable and delicious Caramelized Red Onion Relish year round! Mix with extra-virgin olive oil and use it as a vinaigrette on a salad of lettuce, tomatoes, fresh basil, green onions, and a handful of blueberries.

Sustainable Storage:
Lasts up to 1 year.

Makes: 6 pints

Ingredients

6 large red onions, peeled and sliced very thinly

¾ cup firmly packed light brown sugar

1 tablespoon extra-virgin olive oil

3 cups dry red wine

½ cup balsamic vinegar

½ teaspoon salt

½ teaspoon freshly ground black pepper

1. In a large, heavy nonstick skillet, over medium-high heat, combine onions and brown sugar with olive oil. Cook uncovered for 25 minutes, or until onions turn golden and start to caramelize, stirring frequently.

2. Stir in wine, vinegar, salt, and pepper; bring to a boil over high heat. Reduce heat to low and cook for 15 minutes, or until most of the liquid has evaporated, stirring frequently.

3. Ladle hot relish into sterilized jars, leaving ½" headspace at the top of each jar. Make sure to remove all air bubbles. Wipe rims and place sterilized lid on each jar. Tightly screw on sterilized screw bands, and process in a water-bath canner for 10 minutes.

4. Move the jars to a cooling surface, leaving plenty of space between the jars. Check all the lids when cool, tightening as needed. If any of the jars did not seal, refrigerate or freeze instead.

Sassy Summer Chutney

Preserve these fruits at their peak ripeness for optimal long-lasting and fresh sustainable flavor. This sweet-savory blend can be used as a condiment, side dish, or sauce.

Sustainable Storage:
Lasts up to 1 year when canned or 6–8 months in the freezer.

Makes: 4 pints

Ingredients

1 pound fresh apricots, peeled, pitted, and chopped

1 pound fresh peaches, peeled, pitted, and chopped

1 pound fresh nectarines, peeled, pitted, and chopped

1 pound fresh pears, peeled, pitted, and chopped

2 small seedless oranges, peeled and chopped

2 tablespoons grated fresh ginger

20 medium cloves garlic, peeled and minced

1 cup golden raisins

1 cup dried cranberries

1 cup apple cider vinegar

1 cup firmly packed light brown sugar

3 cups finely diced sweet onions

2 cups orange juice

$\frac{1}{2}$ teaspoon ground cinnamon

$\frac{1}{2}$ teaspoon ground cloves

1 teaspoon salt

$\frac{1}{2}$ teaspoon ground allspice

Sassy Summer Chutney cont.

1. Combine all ingredients in a large pot over medium heat. Bring to a boil, stirring constantly.

2. Reduce heat to low and simmer for 45 minutes, continuing to stir regularly. The chutney will begin to thicken. Remove from heat.

3. Cool and transfer into freezer-safe containers, leaving $\frac{1}{4}$" headspace for expansion. If canning, pack hot mixture into sterilized jars, leaving $\frac{1}{4}$" headspace at the top of each jar. Make sure to remove all air bubbles. Wipe rims and place sterilized lid on each jar. Tightly screw on sterilized screw bands, and process in a water-bath canner for 15 minutes.

4. Move the jars to a cooling surface, leaving plenty of space between the jars. Check all the lids when cool, tightening as needed. If any of the jars did not seal, refrigerate or freeze instead.

Tropical Temptation Salsa

Lower your carbon footprint and ditch store-bought bottled salsa.

Sustainable Storage:
Lasts up to 1 year when canned or 2 months in the freezer.

Makes: about 8 pints

Ingredients

2 cups diced ripe mangoes

2 cups diced ripe pineapple

2 cups diced ripe passion fruit

2 cups diced bell peppers

$\frac{1}{2}$ cup finely chopped onion

$\frac{1}{2}$ teaspoon crushed red pepper flakes

2 teaspoons finely chopped garlic

2 teaspoons grated fresh ginger

2 medium banana peppers, seeded and finely diced

1 cup firmly packed light brown sugar

$1\frac{1}{4}$ cups apple cider vinegar

$\frac{1}{2}$ cup water

1. In a large pot over medium heat, combine all ingredients. Slowly bring to a boil, stirring regularly. Let boil for 5 minutes.

2. Reduce heat to low and simmer another 5 minutes. If freezing, cool and transfer into freezer-safe containers, leaving $\frac{1}{4}$" headspace for expansion.

3. If canning, pack hot mixture into sterilized jars, leaving at least $\frac{1}{2}$" headspace at the top of each jar. Make sure to remove all air bubbles. Wipe rims and place sterilized lid on each jar. Tightly screw on sterilized screw bands, and process in a water-bath canner for 10 minutes.

4. Move the jars to a cooling surface, leaving plenty of space between the jars. Check all the lids when cool, tightening as needed. If any of the jars did not seal, refrigerate or freeze instead.

Preservation Pointers

Many preservers use covered ice cube trays for freezing things like salsa and other sauces in single-serving sizes. In this form, you can pop out what you need and cover the remaining cubes for future use.

Shallot Confiture

This Shallot Confiture will help you become more self-sustainable with an easily preserved condiment that's delicious served with warm or cold meats, or to be applied as a marinade.

Sustainable Storage:
Lasts up to 9 months after allowing flavors to meld for 2–3 months.

Makes: 7 pints

Ingredients

3 pounds shallots, peeled, root ends intact

1 1/2 cups canning salt

8 cups apple cider vinegar

4 1/2 cups granulated sugar

4 cardamom pods, crushed

2 teaspoons dried lemon peel

2 medium cinnamon sticks

4–6 small dried red chili peppers

2 1/2 teaspoons whole cloves

1 tablespoon whole black peppercorns

1/2 cup caraway seeds

1. **Day 1:** Place shallots in a large nonmetallic bowl; sprinkle with canning salt. Add enough water to cover, stirring carefully to dissolve the salt. Put a plate on top of the shallots to submerge them completely. Cover with a clean cotton dish towel; put in a cool place and let sit for 24 hours.

2. **Day 2:** Drain and rinse shallots thoroughly in cool water; dry on paper towels. Pour the vinegar and sugar into a large stockpot; stir well.

3. To make a spice ball, fold a square of cheesecloth twice and place cardamom, lemon peel, cinnamon sticks, chili peppers, cloves, and peppercorns on the surface. Gather up the corners and tie with kitchen string.

4. Add spice ball to the stockpot; pour in the caraway seeds. Heat on medium heat, stirring until sugar has completely dissolved. Raise the heat and bring to a boil; boil for 10 minutes. Add shallots and reduce heat to low. Simmer gently for 15 minutes. Remove stockpot from heat, cover, and let sit for 24 hours.

Continued on next page

Shallot Confiture cont.

5. **Day 3:** Return stockpot to medium heat. Slowly bring shallots to a boil, then reduce heat to low and simmer for 15 minutes. Remove stockpot from heat, cover, and let sit for 24 hours.

6. **Day 4:** Return stockpot to medium heat. Slowly bring shallots to a boil once more, then reduce heat to low. Simmer gently until shallots are golden brown and translucent. Discard spice ball.

7. Pack hot mixture into sterilized jars, leaving $\frac{1}{4}$" headspace at the top of each jar. Make sure to remove all air bubbles. Wipe rims and place sterilized lid on each jar. Tightly screw on sterilized screw bands, and process in a water-bath canner for 10 minutes.

8. Move the jars to a cooling surface, leaving plenty of space between the jars. Check all the lids when cool, tightening as needed. If any of the jars did not seal, refrigerate or freeze instead.

9. Store jars in a cool, dark, dry place for 2–3 months before consuming, to allow flavors to meld.

Asian Vinaigrette

Never rely on store-bought vinaigrettes again. This self-sufficient vinaigrette is good on noodles, as a dipping sauce for dim sum, or as a salad dressing. It comes together very quickly. Refrigerate and shake well before using.

Sustainable Storage: Lasts up to 1 year in the freezer.

Makes: 5–6 pints

Ingredients

1 cup soy sauce

1 cup rice vinegar

1 cup sesame oil

1 cup extra-virgin olive oil

$\frac{1}{4}$ cup honey

4 teaspoons freshly grated orange zest

4 teaspoons ground ginger

2 teaspoons freshly ground black pepper

1 large bunch green onions, trimmed and finely diced

4 teaspoons sesame seeds

1. Whisk all ingredients together in a large saucepan over low heat. Cook for 10 minutes to allow the mixture to reduce.

2. Ladle hot vinaigrette into sterilized jars, leaving $\frac{1}{4}$" headspace at the top of each jar. Make sure to remove all air bubbles. Wipe rims and place sterilized lid on each jar. Tightly screw on sterilized screw bands, and process in a water-bath canner for 15 minutes.

3. Move the jars to a cooling surface, leaving plenty of space between the jars. Check all the lids when cool, tightening as needed. If any of the jars did not seal, refrigerate instead.

Peanut Sauce

This Peanut Sauce is an essential self-sustainable condiment because of its versatility—it's marvelous with chicken, grilled beef, pork, noodles, rice, and even breadsticks. Add more water if you prefer a thinner consistency.

Sustainable Storage:
Lasts 6–8 months.

Makes: 1 cup

Ingredients

1 medium shallot, peeled and minced

1 teaspoon peanut oil

$\frac{1}{4}$ cup peanut butter

2 teaspoons soy sauce

1 teaspoon dark sesame oil

1 teaspoon rice vinegar

1 tablespoon firmly packed light brown sugar or honey

1 medium clove garlic, peeled and crushed

$\frac{1}{2}$ teaspoon ground ginger

$\frac{1}{2}$ teaspoon crushed red pepper flakes, plus more to taste

$\frac{1}{2}$ cup water

1 tablespoon fresh lemon or lime juice

1. In a small saucepan over medium heat sauté shallot in peanut oil until tender. Add remaining ingredients except lemon or lime juice.

2. Whisk over medium heat until mixture comes to a very soft boil. Taste and add more red pepper flakes if desired, then add lemon or lime juice a few drops at a time to balance out the flavors.

3. Cool and transfer into two (half-pint) freezer-safe containers, leaving $\frac{1}{4}$" headspace for expansion, or add to meat as a marinade in an appropriate airtight container. Store in the freezer.

Brown Sauce Sheets

Who said self-sustainable food had to be flavorless? These delicious Brown Sauce Sheets can be sliced and placed over meat while it's cooking or used a little at a time in soups and stews for extra flavor. If you like a sweeter sauce, sprinkle a few pinches of sugar on the onions as they sauté.

Sustainable Storage:
Lasts up to 1 year.

Makes: 5 cups

Ingredients

1 tablespoon extra-virgin olive oil

2 large sweet onions, peeled and roughly chopped

$\frac{1}{2}$ cup tamarind paste

2 tablespoons minced garlic

2 tablespoons grated fresh ginger

$\frac{1}{4}$ cup tomato paste

2 tablespoons freshly ground black pepper

$\frac{1}{2}$ cup dark corn syrup

1 cup blackstrap molasses

2 cups white vinegar

1 cup balsamic vinegar

1 cup dark beer

$\frac{1}{2}$ cup orange juice

$\frac{1}{4}$ cup soy sauce

2 tablespoons coarsely ground yellow mustard seeds

2 tablespoons liquid smoke

2 cups low-fat beef broth

1. In a large skillet, heat olive oil. Add onions and sauté until soft.

2. In a large saucepan over medium heat, combine onions and all remaining ingredients; bring to a boil. Stir regularly.

3. Reduce heat to low and simmer, stirring regularly over the next 2–3 hours until mixture reduces by about 1 cup. Increase simmering time for a thicker sauce with more concentrated flavors.

4. Place an even coating of the sauce on waxed paper or the fruit roll-up sheets of your dehydrator. For the latter, follow the manufacturer's directions for using the dehydrator. If drying in the oven, set the temperature for 150°F; cook until no longer sticky. This can take up to 12 hours, depending on the environment.

5. Slice to preferred sizes. Wrap in waxed paper; store in a jar or food-storage bag in a cool, dry place for future use.

Pickled Ginger Sauce

Take your self-sustainability to the next level and pickle your ginger ahead of time for this recipe instead of buying pickled ginger. This is a wonderful Asian-style dipping sauce that can be canned or frozen. Garnish with chopped green onions when serving, if you like.

Sustainable Storage:
Lasts up to 6 months if canned and up to 4 months in the freezer.

Makes: 2 cups

Ingredients

½ cup rice vinegar

¼ cup fresh lime juice

1 tablespoon dried minced onion

½ tablespoon snipped chives

1 teaspoon freshly ground black pepper

1½ teaspoons minced pickled ginger, plus 1 cup of the pickling juice

1 teaspoon dark soy sauce

1. Combine all ingredients in a medium non-aluminum saucepan over medium heat.

2. Let the sauce come to a low rolling boil; cook until reduced by about ½ cup.

3. If freezing, cool and transfer into freezer-safe containers, leaving ¼" headspace for expansion. If canning, pack hot mixture into sterilized jars, leaving ¼" headspace at the top of each jar. Make sure to remove all air bubbles. Wipe rims and place sterilized lid on each jar. Tightly screw on sterilized screw bands, and process in a water-bath canner for 35 minutes.

4. Move the jars to a cooling surface, leaving plenty of space between the jars. Check all the lids when cool, tightening as needed. If any of the jars did not seal, refrigerate or freeze instead.

Pickled Dressing

If you want to maximize its sustainability and can this Pickled Dressing, leave out the Parmesan cheese and add fresh cheese when you're ready to serve the dressing.

Sustainable Storage:
Lasts up to 1 year when canned or 6 months in the freezer.

Makes: 2 cups

Ingredients

1 cup red wine vinegar

$\frac{1}{2}$ cup granulated sugar

5 teaspoons kosher salt

$\frac{1}{4}$ cup extra-virgin olive oil

$\frac{1}{4}$ cup chopped fresh basil

2 medium cloves garlic, peeled and pressed

1$\frac{1}{2}$ tablespoons grated Parmesan cheese

2 teaspoons sweet pimento, finely chopped

1. In a medium saucepan, whisk together all ingredients except cheese and pimento. Place over low heat and bring to a boil.

2. Remove from heat. Stir in cheese (if freezing rather than canning) and pimento.

3. If freezing, cool and transfer into freezer-safe containers, leaving $\frac{1}{4}$" headspace for expansion. If canning, pour hot dressing into sterilized jar, leaving $\frac{1}{4}$" headspace at the top. Make sure to remove all air bubbles. Wipe rim and place sterilized lid on the jar. Tightly screw on sterilized screw band, and process in a water-bath canner for 15 minutes.

4. Move the jar to a cooling surface. Check the lid when cool, tightening as needed. If the jar did not seal, refrigerate or freeze instead.

CHAPTER SEVEN

Marinades and Sauces

Burnt Onion Concentrate

Make this recipe in bulk for a ready-to-eat sauce or marinade. It's also great for flavoring gravies, soups, and stews.

Sustainable Storage:
Lasts up to 1 year.

Makes: 8 pints

Ingredients

3 pounds onions, peeled and coarsely chopped

7½ cups cold water

3 cups firmly packed dark brown sugar

7½ cups apple cider vinegar

3 tablespoons dried French tarragon

1 teaspoon salt

1 teaspoon coarsely ground black pepper

1. In a large stockpot over medium heat, combine onions and water. Cover and bring to a boil. Reduce heat to low and simmer until onions are soft. Add sugar; stir well to dissolve.

2. Continue to simmer uncovered, stirring occasionally to prevent sticking, until mixture has turned a very dark brown and has reduced by about half, at least 1 hour.

3. In a separate medium saucepan, over medium heat, combine vinegar, tarragon, salt, and pepper. Bring to a boil. Reduce heat to low and simmer uncovered for 10 minutes.

4. Slowly pour vinegar mixture into onion mixture; stir well. Raise heat to medium and bring to a boil; reduce heat to low and simmer for 10 minutes.

5. Ladle into sterilized jars, leaving 1" headspace at the top of each jar. Make sure to remove all air bubbles. Wipe rims and place sterilized lid on each jar. Tightly screw on sterilized screw bands, and process in a water-bath canner for 10 minutes.

Buffalo Chicken Marinade

This marinade is great to keep on hand in your pantry since it's great with any poultry, makes a zesty grilling blend for vegetables, and can be adapted to marinate beef—simply substitute red wine and red wine vinegar for the white wine and the apple cider vinegar, respectively.

Sustainable Storage:
Lasts up to 1 year.

Makes: 2 pints

Ingredients

$4\frac{1}{8}$ cups apple cider vinegar

2 cups extra-virgin olive oil

$\frac{1}{2}$ cup dry white wine

1 tablespoon hot sauce

3 teaspoons salt

1 teaspoon granulated sugar

1 teaspoon fresh lemon juice

1 teaspoon freshly ground black pepper

1 teaspoon paprika

$\frac{1}{4}$ teaspoon ground cayenne pepper

$\frac{1}{4}$ teaspoon garlic powder

$\frac{1}{4}$ teaspoon onion powder

$\frac{1}{4}$ teaspoon ground dried oregano

$\frac{1}{4}$ teaspoon ground dried thyme

$\frac{1}{4}$ teaspoon ground dried sage

$\frac{1}{4}$ teaspoon ground dried basil

$\frac{1}{4}$ teaspoon dried rosemary

1 dried bay leaf

1. In a medium saucepan over medium heat, combine all ingredients. Bring to a boil and maintain a low rolling boil until marinade reduces by about $\frac{1}{2}$ cup.

2. Pour into sterilized jars, leaving $\frac{1}{2}$" headspace at the top of each jar. Make sure to remove all air bubbles. Wipe rims and place sterilized lid on each jar. Tightly screw on sterilized screw bands, and process in a water-bath canner for 15 minutes.

3. Move the jars to a cooling surface, leaving plenty of space between the jars. Check all the lids when cool, tightening as needed. If any of the jars did not seal, refrigerate or freeze instead.

Preservation Pointers

The best tenderizing marinades are those that have ingredients with a high acid content. The acid helps relax protein in meat, making it tender. In the process, the flavors of these items penetrate the food.

All-Purpose Dry Marinade

Simply sprinkle 1–2 teaspoons on each side of your meat, poultry, fish, or vegetables, and let sit. Meat and poultry improve from a full day in the refrigerator with the dry marinade rubbed in. Fish and vegetables can go on the stove or grill almost immediately.

Sustainable Storage:
Lasts up to 1 year.

Makes: $1\frac{1}{2}$ cups

Ingredients

1 medium onion, peeled and diced

5 medium cloves garlic, peeled and diced

$\frac{1}{4}$ cup chopped fresh oregano

$\frac{1}{4}$ cup chopped fresh chives

1 medium orange, peel carefully removed without pith and reserved

1 medium lemon, peel carefully removed without pith and reserved

1–2 medium chili peppers, seeded and diced

$\frac{1}{3}$ cup firmly packed light brown sugar

$\frac{1}{3}$ cup paprika

$\frac{1}{3}$ cup salt

$\frac{1}{3}$ cup whole peppercorns

2 tablespoons mustard powder

2 tablespoons Worcestershire sauce

1. You will use either your oven or a dehydrator to dry the vegetables. If using your oven, lightly grease four baking sheets with oil.

2. Place the onion, garlic, oregano, and chives, evenly spaced, on a tray in the dehydrator or on a prepared baking sheet.

3. Place the orange and lemon peels on a second tray or baking sheet.

4. Finely dice the lemon and orange; place on a third tray or baking sheet.

5. Place chili pepper on a fourth tray or baking sheet.

6. If using the oven, place the baking sheets in the oven and set the temperature at 150°F. The mixture will dry in about 2 hours, but make sure that everything is crunchy (not rubbery). Any rubbery items should remain in the heat until fully dried. If using a dehydrator, follow the manufacturer's recommended time and temperature guidelines, drying foods longer if the items aren't fully crunchy.

7. Place all the freshly dried goods in a spice grinder and grind to a consistent texture. In a small bowl, combine ground dried goods with remaining ingredients; mix well. Store in an airtight container in a cool, dark area.

Raspberry Reduction Marinade

Feel free to experiment with different types of juiced fruits.

Sustainable Storage:
Lasts up to 8 months.

Makes: 5 cups

Ingredients

1 medium red onion, peeled and minced

1 teaspoon extra-virgin olive oil

2 cups raspberry juice

2 cups dry red wine

$\frac{1}{2}$ cup low-fat beef broth

$\frac{1}{2}$ cup golden raisins

$\frac{1}{2}$ cup raspberry vinegar

2 tablespoons grated fresh ginger

$\frac{1}{4}$ cup granulated sugar

1 tablespoon Dijon mustard

1. In a large skillet over medium heat, gently sauté onion in olive oil until golden brown. Add remaining ingredients to the skillet and bring to a simmer. Cook until liquid reduces by about 1 cup; remove from heat.

2. Cool and transfer into freezer-safe containers, leaving $\frac{1}{4}$" headspace for expansion, or pour over meat and freeze everything together.

South of the Border Beef Marinade

This is the perfect marinade to stock up on for taco night. Don't forget a side of refried beans!

Sustainable Storage:
Lasts up to 8 months.

Makes: 2 cups

Ingredients

$\frac{1}{2}$ cup fresh lime juice

$\frac{1}{2}$ cup chopped fresh cilantro

$\frac{1}{2}$ cup extra-virgin olive oil

$\frac{1}{3}$ cup soy sauce

$\frac{1}{2}$ cup tequila

7 medium cloves garlic, peeled and finely chopped

2 teaspoons freshly grated lime zest

2 teaspoons freshly grated orange zest

2 teaspoons ground cumin

2 teaspoons dried oregano

1 teaspoon freshly ground black pepper

1. In a medium saucepan over low heat, combine all ingredients. Cook until mixture reaches a gentle boil.

2. Cool and transfer into freezer-safe containers, leaving $\frac{1}{4}$" headspace for expansion.

Ginger Citrus Marinade

This diet-friendly marinade is great to have on hand. Use this on chicken and pork, marinating the meat for at least 2 hours before cooking.

Sustainable Storage:
Lasts up to 1 year.

Makes: 4 cups

Ingredients

1 medium lemon, juiced and zested

1 medium lime, juiced and zested

3 cups orange juice

1 teaspoon freshly grated orange zest

$\frac{1}{2}$ cup water

2 tablespoons white vinegar

3 teaspoons grated fresh ginger

3 teaspoons grated sweet onion

2 teaspoons freshly ground black pepper

1. In a medium saucepan over medium heat, combine lemon juice, lime juice, orange juice, and orange zest; add 1 teaspoon lemon zest and 1 teaspoon lime zest. Discard any remaining zest.

2. Add water, vinegar, ginger, onion, and pepper. Bring to a low rolling boil, stirring regularly, and continue cooking until mixture reduces by $\frac{1}{4}$ cup.

3. Pour into sterilized jars, leaving $\frac{1}{2}$" headspace at the top of each jar. Make sure to remove all air bubbles. Wipe rims and place sterilized lid on each jar. Tightly screw on sterilized screw bands, and process in a water-bath canner for 15 minutes.

4. Move the jars to a cooling surface, leaving plenty of space between the jars. Check all the lids when cool, tightening as needed. If any of the jars did not seal, refrigerate or freeze instead.

Asian Plum Sauce

If you don't have plums on hand, make this sauce with peaches or tangerines.

Sustainable Storage:
Lasts up to 1 year.

Makes: 6–7 pints

Ingredients

1 cup granulated sugar

1½ cups firmly packed light
   brown sugar

1 cup apple cider vinegar

¾ cup finely chopped onion

2 tablespoons whole yellow
   mustard seeds

2 tablespoons finely chopped
   green chilies

1 tablespoon salt

1–2 medium cloves garlic,
   peeled and minced

1–2 medium pieces fresh ginger,
   peeled and minced

10 cups finely chopped
   pitted plums

1. In a large stockpot over medium heat, combine granulated sugar, brown sugar, vinegar, onion, mustard seeds, chilies, salt, garlic, and ginger.

2. Bring to a boil; add plums.

3. Return mixture to a boil. Boil gently, stirring occasionally, about 1 hour 45 minutes, or until thick and syrupy.

4. Ladle into sterilized jars, leaving ¼" headspace at the top of each jar. Make sure to remove all air bubbles. Wipe rims and place sterilized lid on each jar. Tightly screw on sterilized screw bands, and process in a water-bath canner for 10 minutes.

5. Move the jars to a cooling surface, leaving plenty of space between the jars. Check all the lids when cool, tightening as needed. If any of the jars did not seal, refrigerate or freeze instead.

Green Taco Sauce

Keep this sauce in your pantry at all times to kick up nearly any Mexican-style dish.

Sustainable Storage:
Lasts up to 1 year.

Makes: 6 pints

Ingredients

2 pounds tomatillos, husked, stemmed, and quartered

4 medium jalapeño peppers, seeded and roughly chopped

1 cup chopped red onion

1 cup chopped shallots

4 teaspoons minced garlic

2 cups fresh cilantro leaves

$\frac{1}{4}$ cup extra-virgin olive oil

4 cups chicken broth

2 cups red wine vinegar

$\frac{1}{2}$ cup honey

1. Bring a large saucepan of water to a boil over high heat. Drop tomatillos in boiling water; cook for 10 minutes. Drain.

2. In a food processor, combine tomatillos, jalapeños, onion, shallots, garlic, and cilantro; pulse until coarse. This may have to be done in 2 or 3 batches.

3. Heat the olive oil in a large stockpot over medium heat. Add the processed vegetables; cook for 5 minutes, stirring constantly.

4. Add the broth, vinegar, and honey; stir well. Reduce heat to low and simmer until thickened, about 20–25 minutes.

5. Ladle into sterilized jars, leaving $\frac{1}{4}$" headspace at the top of each jar. Make sure to remove all air bubbles. Wipe rims and place sterilized lid on each jar. Tightly screw on sterilized screw bands, and process at 10 pounds of pressure in a pressure canner for 20 minutes.

6. Move the jars to a cooling surface, leaving plenty of space between the jars. Check all the lids when cool, tightening as needed. If any of the jars did not seal, refrigerate or freeze instead.

Ho-Ho Hot Sauce

This hot sauce is high in both heat and flavor and offers a smooth finish. This recipe can also be canned from the liquid stage.

Sustainable Storage:
Lasts up to 1 year.

Makes: 1 cup powdered red sauce, or about 2 cups canned

Ingredients

2 medium cayenne peppers, cut in half and seeded

2 medium habanero peppers, cut in half and seeded

2 medium banana peppers, cut in half and seeded

2 medium jalapeño peppers, cut in half and seeded

2 medium Scotch bonnet peppers, cut in half and seeded

2 medium Anaheim peppers, cut in half and seeded

1 medium red bell pepper, cut in half and seeded

1 medium orange bell pepper, cut in half and seeded

$\frac{1}{4}$ cup diced onion

1 teaspoon extra-virgin olive oil

3 medium cloves garlic, peeled and finely chopped

1 teaspoon grated fresh ginger

$\frac{1}{2}$ cup white vinegar

1 tablespoon dark molasses

2 tablespoons honey

2 tablespoons orange juice

2 tablespoons firmly packed dark brown sugar

1 medium Roma tomato, cored and chopped

$\frac{1}{4}$ cup spiced dark rum

$\frac{1}{2}$ teaspoon chipotle powder

$\frac{1}{2}$ teaspoon curry powder

$\frac{1}{2}$ teaspoon salt

$\frac{1}{2}$ teaspoon freshly ground black pepper

Continued on next page

Ho-Ho Hot Sauce cont.

1. Line a dehydrator tray with parchment paper or nonstick silicone sheets.

2. Roast all peppers skin side up under the broiler or on the grill until blackened. Remove skins.

3. In a large saucepan over medium-low heat, sauté onion in olive oil until translucent. Remove from heat.

4. Working in batches if necessary, process peppers in a food processor, pulsing to achieve an even puréed consistency.

5. Return saucepan with onion to low heat. Add processed peppers and remaining ingredients and simmer for 5 minutes, stirring regularly.

6. Run the mixture through a sieve, then return to the saucepan over low heat to simmer another 10 minutes. If canning, leave $1/4$" headspace and process in a water-bath canner for 35 minutes. If dehydrating, remove from heat and cool to room temperature.

7. Pour $1/4$ cup sauce evenly over the surface of lined dehydrator tray. Place in dehydrator, using manufacturer's suggested setting for drying herbs.

8. Check after 1 hour; if peppers have reached a rubbery stage, peel the mixture off the tray. Allow to cool. Dice mixture and run through an herb grinder.

9. Return ground pieces to the dehydrator for 1 hour, until crunchy. Put through herb grinder again.

10. Store in airtight container in a cool, dark area.

11. Repeat steps 7–10 for the rest of the mix, or put into a jar and store in the refrigerator for immediate use.

Honey Barbecue Sauce

Feel free to adapt this recipe to your family's tastes as you stock up on your own classic barbecue sauce. If you prefer a maple-flavored barbecue sauce, use maple syrup in place of honey.

Sustainable Storage:
Lasts 6–8 months.

Makes: 6–7 pints

Ingredients

20 pounds firm ripe tomatoes, cored and chopped

4 large onions, peeled and finely chopped

6–8 medium cloves garlic, peeled and minced

$1\frac{1}{4}$ tablespoons crushed red pepper flakes

2 tablespoons celery seeds

2 cups firmly packed dark brown sugar

1 cup honey

2 tablespoons dry mustard

2 teaspoons salt

$1\frac{1}{2}$ teaspoons ground mace

$1\frac{1}{2}$ teaspoons ground ginger

$1\frac{1}{2}$ teaspoons ground cinnamon

$\frac{1}{2}$ teaspoon freshly grated orange zest

2 cups white vinegar

$\frac{2}{3}$ cup fresh lemon juice

1 teaspoon freshly ground black pepper

1. In a large stockpot over low heat, combine tomatoes, onions, garlic, red pepper flakes, and celery seeds. Simmer, covered, until vegetables are soft, about 30 minutes.

2. Press tomato mixture through a fine sieve or food mill; discard seeds and skins.

3. Return tomato mixture to stockpot; add remaining ingredients.

4. Cook over low heat, stirring frequently, until mixture thickens, about 60–90 minutes.

5. Cool; ladle sauce into freezer-safe containers, leaving $\frac{1}{4}$" headspace for expansion.

Preservation Pointers

In cooking, there are several sauces known as mother sauces (or grand sauces)—tomato or red sauce; hollandaise or butter sauce; espagnole or brown sauce; velouté or blond sauce; and béchamel or white sauce. They get this designation because once you know how to make them, you'll know the fundamental process for all other sauces.

Pickled Onion Sauce

Use herbs you have on hand for this recipe if you don't have celery and mustard seeds. Other herbs worth trying in this blend include cumin, ginger, and allspice. Stock up to enjoy with bratwurst, garlic sausage, and kielbasa.

Sustainable Storage:
Lasts up to 8 months.

Makes: 3 cups

Ingredients

1 large red onion, peeled, thinly sliced, and blanched for 2 minutes

2 medium chili peppers, seeded, diced, and blanched for 2 minutes

10 medium cloves garlic, peeled and chopped

1½ cups white vinegar

½ cup granulated sugar

1 tablespoon whole yellow mustard seeds

1 tablespoon celery seeds

½ cup dark beer

¼ cup dark honey

1 teaspoon salt

1. In a medium saucepan over medium-high heat, combine all ingredients. Bring to a boil.

2. Reduce heat to low and simmer until sauce reduces by $\frac{1}{4}$ cup.

3. Cool to room temperature. Run mixture through a blender or food processor until it is a smooth, consistent texture.

4. Transfer to freezer-safe containers, leaving $\frac{1}{4}$" headspace for expansion.

Apple Maple Sauce

This reduction is delicious on ham and pork. If you want to cut down on prep time, substitute 1 1/2 cups applesauce for the fresh apples.

Sustainable Storage:
Lasts up to 1 year.

Makes: 3 cups

Ingredients

4 large firm apples, cored and diced

2 whole cloves

1 teaspoon red wine vinegar

1/2 cup real maple syrup

1/4 cup prepared apple jelly

2 teaspoons minced garlic

1 cup low-fat chicken broth

1. In a medium saucepan, combine apples and cloves; add enough water to cover.

2. Simmer over low heat, stirring regularly until apples are soft.

3. Put the apple mixture through a sieve. Return applesauce to saucepan and add remaining ingredients.

4. Bring to a rolling boil over medium-high heat, stirring regularly. Allow liquid to reduce by 1/2 cup.

5. Pour into sterilized jars, leaving 1/4" headspace at the top of each jar. Make sure to remove all air bubbles. Wipe rims and place sterilized lid on each jar. Tightly screw on sterilized screw bands, and process in a water-bath canner for 15 minutes.

6. Move the jars to a cooling surface, leaving plenty of space between the jars. Check all the lids when cool, tightening as needed. If any of the jars did not seal, refrigerate or freeze instead.

English Mint Sauce

If you have a garden, this is the perfect recipe to use your own freshly grown mint.

Sustainable Storage:
Lasts up to 6 months.

Makes: 6 pints

Ingredients

4 cups finely chopped fresh mint

4 cups granulated sugar

$\frac{1}{3}$ cup fresh lemon or lime juice

2 (12-ounce) bottles malt vinegar

2 cups white vinegar

1. Add all ingredients to a large stockpot over medium heat. Bring to a boil, then reduce heat to low and simmer until mint leaves are softened.

2. Ladle hot sauce into sterilized jars, leaving 1" headspace at the top of each jar. Make sure to remove all air bubbles. Wipe rims and place sterilized lid on each jar. Tightly screw on sterilized screw bands, and process in a water-bath canner for 15 minutes.

3. Move the jars to a cooling surface, leaving plenty of space between the jars. Check all the lids when cool, tightening as needed. If any of the jars did not seal, refrigerate or freeze instead.

Apricot Baste

This recipe can add flavor to pretty much anything.

Sustainable Storage:
Lasts up to 6 months.

Makes: $1\frac{1}{2}$ cups

Ingredients

3 medium cloves garlic, peeled and minced

1 teaspoon sesame seeds

2 teaspoons sesame oil

$\frac{1}{3}$ cup diced dried apricots

$\frac{1}{2}$ cup prepared apricot preserves

1 tablespoon soy sauce

1 tablespoon coarsely ground yellow mustard seeds

1 cup apricot nectar

1 tablespoon orange-blossom honey

1 tablespoon rice vinegar

1 teaspoon orange flower water

1. In a medium saucepan over medium heat, lightly toast garlic and sesame seeds in sesame oil. Add all remaining ingredients except orange flower water.

2. Bring to a simmer and let the mixture reduce by $\frac{1}{4}$ cup. Remove from heat and allow to cool to room temperature; stir in orange flower water.

3. Transfer into freezer-safe containers, leaving $\frac{1}{4}$" headspace for expansion.

Spiced Tomato Paste

Stock up on this classic Spiced Tomato Paste instead of a store-bought version. This recipe uses a dehydrator to make tomato paste roll-ups that are best either kept in an airtight container in a dark, cool place or well wrapped in the freezer. Rehydrate the paste as needed.

Sustainable Storage:
Lasts up to 1 year.

Makes: 12 paste roll-ups

Ingredients

4 pounds ripe Roma tomatoes

1 teaspoon dried oregano

$\frac{1}{2}$ cup finely diced onion

$\frac{1}{4}$ teaspoon garlic powder

1 teaspoon pressed garlic

1 teaspoon fresh chopped basil

$\frac{1}{3}$ cup dry white wine

1. Line a dehydrator tray with a nonstick silicone sheet. Lightly oil the sheet, or use parchment paper.

2. Dice the tomatoes and put them through a food processor. Press them through a sieve to remove the seeds.

3. Add tomatoes and remaining ingredients to a large saucepan over low heat. Simmer, stirring occasionally, about 30 minutes or until the consistency thickens and becomes paste-like.

4. Spread the paste on lined dehydrator tray. Paste should be no more than $\frac{1}{4}$" thick.

5. Dry at about 115°F–120°F for 12 hours or until the paste is not sticky. Store as desired.

CHAPTER EIGHT

Broths, Soups, and Stews

Lamb Broth

Keeping lamb broth in your pantry is essential if you enjoy Greek food. It's also great when making bean casseroles or when basting chops and full legs of lamb.

Sustainable Storage:
Lasts up to 1 year.

Makes: 14–16 quarts

Ingredients

$\frac{1}{3}$ cup extra-virgin olive oil, divided

3–4 medium (5-pound) lamb shanks, divided

2 pounds lamb stew meat (with bones), divided

8 cups beef broth, divided

2 pounds carrots, peeled and cut into large chunks, divided

2 cups celery, trimmed and cut into chunks, divided

2 large onions, peeled and diced, divided

2 tablespoons mixed whole peppercorns, divided

1 tablespoon whole allspice berries, divided

$\frac{1}{4}$ cup dried mixed soup greens, divided

8 dried bay leaves, divided

2 tablespoons dried oregano, divided

2 teaspoons Greek seasoning, divided

6 lamb or beef bouillon cubes, divided

Lamb Broth cont.

1. Divide olive oil evenly between two large stockpots. Add lamb shanks and stew meat, dividing between the stockpots.

2. Over medium-high heat, cook lamb until evenly browned.

3. Add 4 cups beef broth per stockpot; reduce heat to low and simmer for 15 minutes.

4. Divide the carrots, celery, and onions evenly between the stockpots.

5. To make two spice balls, fold two squares of cheesecloth twice. Divide the peppercorns, allspice berries, mixed soup greens, and bay leaves evenly between the two pieces of cheesecloth. Gather up the corners and tie with kitchen string. Add one spice ball to each stockpot.

6. Add enough cold water to each stockpot to cover lamb. Bring to a rapid boil over medium heat; cover, reduce heat to low, and simmer for 3 hours.

7. Skim off and discard any foam and fat from the surface of the broth. Divide oregano, Greek seasoning, and bouillon evenly between the two stockpots. Cook on low for another 15 minutes.

8. If canning, strain and ladle into sterilized jars, leaving 1" headspace at the top of each jar. Make sure to remove all air bubbles. Wipe rims and place sterilized lid on each jar. Tightly screw on sterilized screw bands, and process at 10 pounds of pressure in a pressure canner for 20 minutes for pints or 25 minutes for quarts.

9. Move the jars to a cooling surface, leaving plenty of space between the jars. Check all the lids when cool, tightening as needed. If any of the jars did not seal, refrigerate or freeze instead.

Dill Pickle Soup Broth

Keep this broth on hand to use as a base for Pickled Soup (see recipe later in this chapter) when you want it.

Sustainable Storage:
Lasts up to 1 year canned or up to 3 months in the freezer.

Makes: 3 cups

Ingredients

3 cups vegetable broth

$\frac{1}{2}$ cup dill pickle brine

3 large cucumber pickles, diced

1 medium onion, peeled and chopped

2 medium carrots, peeled and chopped

1. In a large stockpot, combine all ingredients over medium heat. Cook until broth reduces by $\frac{1}{2}$ cup.

2. Strain broth. If freezing, cool and transfer into freezer-safe containers, leaving $\frac{1}{4}$" headspace for expansion. If canning, pour into sterilized jars, leaving 1" headspace at the top of each jar. Make sure to remove all air bubbles. Wipe rims and place sterilized lid on each jar. Tightly screw on sterilized screw bands, and process at 10 pounds of pressure in a pressure canner for 25 minutes for pints.

3. Move the jars to a cooling surface, leaving plenty of space between the jars. Check all the lids when cool, tightening as needed. If any of the jars did not seal, refrigerate or freeze instead.

Shellfish Broth

Having this Shellfish Broth handy is great for when you're craving some homemade crab or lobster bisque.

Sustainable Storage:
Lasts up to 1 year.

Makes: 4 quarts

Ingredients

2 tablespoons unsalted butter

2 large onions, peeled and chopped

1 bunch leeks, trimmed and chopped

4–5 medium cloves garlic, peeled and chopped

3–4 medium stalks celery, chopped

1 pound carrots, peeled and roughly chopped

4–5 pounds lobster or crab shells

$\frac{1}{4}$ cup fresh lemon juice

$\frac{1}{2}$ cup chopped fresh parsley

1 teaspoon whole black peppercorns

3–4 dried bay leaves

$\frac{1}{2}$ teaspoon dried basil

$\frac{1}{2}$ teaspoon dried oregano

$\frac{1}{2}$ teaspoon dried tarragon

$\frac{1}{2}$ teaspoon dried thyme

1 cup dry white wine

1 gallon cold water

1. In a large stockpot over medium heat, melt butter; add onions, leeks, garlic, and celery, and sauté about 5 minutes, or until soft.

2. Add remaining ingredients; simmer about 1 hour. Periodically skim off foam that will appear at top of pot.

3. Remove from heat and strain broth. Ladle hot broth into sterilized jars, leaving 1" headspace at the top of each jar. Make sure to remove all air bubbles. Wipe rims and place sterilized lid on each jar. Tightly screw on sterilized screw bands, and process at 10 pounds of pressure in a pressure canner for 30 minutes for pints or 35 minutes for quarts.

4. Move the jars to a cooling surface, leaving plenty of space between the jars. Check all the lids when cool, tightening as needed. If any of the jars did not seal, refrigerate or freeze instead.

Ham Broth

This recipe is so simple and delicious that you'll want to make it in bulk. Try this broth the next time you make scalloped potatoes and ham. Garnish with a bit of melted cheese.

Sustainable Storage:
Lasts up to 1 year when canned or 3–4 months in the freezer.

Makes: 4 cups

Ingredients

2 pounds ham, with ham bone

5 cups water

1 large carrot, peeled and sliced into large chunks

1 large onion, peeled and quartered

2 medium stalks celery, coarsely diced, with leaves

$\frac{1}{2}$ teaspoon crushed dried parsley

$\frac{1}{2}$ teaspoon celery seeds

$\frac{1}{2}$ teaspoon onion powder

1 bay leaf

1. In a large stockpot, combine all ingredients over low heat. Cover and simmer for 40 minutes.

2. Uncover the pot and allow mixture to reduce by 1 cup. Strain broth; discard residue. Cool; skim off fat.

3. If freezing, transfer into freezer-safe containers, leaving $\frac{1}{4}$" headspace for expansion. If canning, pour into sterilized jars, leaving 1" headspace at the top of each jar. Make sure to remove all air bubbles. Wipe rims and place sterilized lid on each jar. Tightly screw on sterilized screw bands, and process at 11 pounds of pressure in a pressure canner for 25 minutes for pints or 30 minutes for quarts.

4. Move the jars to a cooling surface, leaving plenty of space between the jars. Check all the lids when cool, tightening as needed. If any of the jars did not seal, refrigerate or freeze instead.

Garlic Broth

Keeping this Garlic Broth ready when you need it means adding richness to all your favorite soups and stews. For a milder garlic taste, roast the garlic in the oven before using it for the broth.

Sustainable Storage: Lasts up to 1 year when canned or up to 6 months in the freezer.

Makes: 6 cups

Ingredients

$1\frac{1}{2}$ tablespoons extra-virgin olive oil

$\frac{1}{2}$ medium head garlic, cloves separated, peeled, and chopped

$\frac{1}{2}$ head elephant garlic, cloves separated, peeled, and chopped

6 cups vegetable broth

1 dried bay leaf

$\frac{1}{4}$ teaspoon dried thyme

$\frac{1}{8}$ teaspoon dried sage

$\frac{1}{8}$ teaspoon salt

$\frac{1}{8}$ teaspoon freshly ground black pepper

1. In a large pot, heat oil over medium heat, and very lightly sauté all chopped garlic.

2. Add all remaining ingredients to the pot; bring to a boil.

3. Reduce heat to low and simmer for 30 minutes.

4. Strain broth; taste and adjust seasonings if needed.

5. Pour into sterilized pint jars, leaving 1" headspace at the top of each jar. Make sure to remove all air bubbles. Wipe rims and place sterilized lid on each jar. Tightly screw on sterilized screw bands, and process at 10 pounds of pressure in a pressure canner for 30 minutes for pints.

6. Move the jars to a cooling surface, leaving plenty of space between the jars. Check all the lids when cool, tightening as needed. If any of the jars did not seal, refrigerate or freeze instead.

Traditional Beef Broth

The red wine in this recipe is optional, but it is an excellent touch if you plan to use the broth for gravies or reductions.

Sustainable Storage:
Lasts up to 1 year.

Makes: 4 quarts

Ingredients

3 pounds shank or pot roast, cut into 2" pieces

2 pounds marrow bones, smashed

1 medium onion, peeled and diced

1 tablespoon extra-virgin olive oil

$\frac{1}{4}$ cup red wine

$\frac{1}{4}$ teaspoon salt

$\frac{1}{4}$ teaspoon freshly ground black pepper

2 medium cloves garlic, peeled

1 cup celery leaves

1. Cook beef under the broiler to medium-well, or as desired. Put into a large stockpot along with marrow bones.

2. In a small skillet over medium heat, sauté onion in olive oil until translucent. Add to stockpot. Add wine, salt, pepper, garlic, and celery leaves. Add enough water to cover, about 12 cups.

3. Set the stockpot over medium heat. Bring broth to a simmer and cook for at least $2\frac{1}{2}$ hours. If necessary, add water during the process to keep bones covered.

4. Cool broth and strain, skimming off as much fat as possible; then return broth to medium heat to heat through.

5. If canning, pour into sterilized jars, leaving 1" headspace at the top of each jar. Make sure to remove all air bubbles. Wipe rims and place sterilized lid on each jar. Tightly screw on sterilized screw bands, and process at 11 pounds of pressure in a pressure canner for 25 minutes.

6. Move the jars to a cooling surface, leaving plenty of space between the jars. Check all the lids when cool, tightening as needed. If any of the jars did not seal, refrigerate or freeze instead.

Classic Chicken Broth

Keeping enough chicken broth in your pantry is advice that goes without saying—ditch the overprocessed store-bought version and preserve your own!

Sustainable Storage: Lasts up to 1 year when canned or 6 months in the freezer.

Makes: 1 quart

Ingredients

2 pounds boneless chicken, cut up in pieces

1 tablespoon extra-virgin olive oil

2⅛ teaspoons salt, divided

⅛ teaspoon freshly ground black pepper

1 medium onion, peeled and diced

1 quart water

2 dried bay leaves

½ teaspoon poultry seasoning

1. In a large skillet over medium heat, combine chicken with olive oil, ⅛ teaspoon salt, and pepper. Cook until chicken is browned. Reserve juices and set aside.

2. In a large stockpot over medium-low heat, combine remaining ingredients. Simmer for 30 minutes, then add the chicken with juices.

3. Bring to a low rolling boil, skimming the fat off regularly.

4. Cool in the refrigerator. Remove any remaining fat once it separates from the broth.

5. If freezing, transfer into freezer-safe containers, leaving ¼" headspace for expansion. If canning, reheat the broth, then ladle into sterilized quart jars, leaving 1" headspace at the top of each jar. Make sure to remove all air bubbles. Wipe rims and place sterilized lid on each jar. Tightly screw on sterilized screw bands, and process at 11 pounds of pressure in a pressure canner for 25 minutes for quarts.

6. Move the jars to a cooling surface, leaving plenty of space between the jars. Check all the lids when cool, tightening as needed. If any of the jars did not seal, refrigerate or freeze instead.

Vegetable Broth

When you're going to be making Vegetable Broth, prepare ahead of time. Keep your clean vegetable ends and pieces in a food-storage bag in the freezer and add them to the broth water for increased flavor.

Sustainable Storage:
Lasts up to 1 year.

Makes: 8 quarts

Ingredients

14 quarts cold water

2 pounds carrots, peeled and cut into 1" pieces

2 pounds parsnips, peeled and cut into 1" pieces

1 bunch leeks, trimmed and chopped finely

12 stalks celery, trimmed and cut into 1" pieces

3 large onions, peeled and quartered

4 large red bell peppers, seeded and cut into 1" pieces

4 large tomatoes, seeded and diced

4 medium turnips, peeled and diced

6 medium cloves garlic, peeled and minced

6 dried bay leaves

2 teaspoons dried thyme

1 cup fresh chopped parsley

1 tablespoon whole black peppercorns

2 teaspoons salt

1. In a large stockpot over medium-high heat, combine all ingredients. Bring to a boil.

2. Cover and reduce heat to low. Simmer for 2 hours.

3. Uncover and simmer for 2 additional hours to concentrate flavors.

4. Strain broth through several layers of cheesecloth in a colander. Discard solids.

5. Ladle broth into sterilized jars, leaving 1" headspace at the top of each jar. Make sure to remove all air bubbles. Wipe rims and place sterilized lid on each jar. Tightly screw on sterilized screw bands, and process at 10 pounds of pressure in a pressure canner for 30 minutes for pints or 35 minutes for quarts.

6. Move the jars to a cooling surface, leaving plenty of space between the jars. Check all the lids when cool, tightening as needed. If any of the jars did not seal, refrigerate or freeze instead.

Ukrainian Cabbage Soup

There's nothing like the comfort of having home-cooked soup preserved for when you want it. You can thicken the soup before freezing or after defrosting by making a butter and flour roux.

Sustainable Storage:
Lasts up to 1 year when canned or 4–6 months in the freezer.

Makes: 7–8 quarts

Ingredients

5–6 pounds pork neck bones

2 dried bay leaves

2 teaspoons freshly ground black pepper

1 large head cabbage, cored and shredded

2 (28-ounce) cans sauerkraut with juice

2 large onions, peeled and finely chopped

4 tablespoons whole caraway seeds

1. Put neck bones in a large stockpot. Add bay leaves and pepper, and enough water to cover. Heat over high heat to bring to a boil; reduce heat to low and simmer for 1 hour.

2. Add cabbage, sauerkraut (including juices), and onions. Continue to cook about 45 minutes; meat will start falling off bones.

3. Add caraway seeds. Remove and discard bay leaves. Remove bones with slotted spoon and allow to sit until cool enough to handle. Remove meat from bones and add meat back into soup. Discard bones.

4. If freezing, cool and transfer into freezer-safe containers, leaving $\frac{1}{4}$" headspace for expansion. If canning, ladle soup into sterilized wide-mouth quart jars, leaving 1" headspace at the top of each jar. Make sure to remove all air bubbles. Wipe rims and place sterilized lid on each jar. Tightly screw on sterilized screw bands, and process in a pressure canner at 10 pounds of pressure for 65 minutes.

5. Move the jars to a cooling surface, leaving plenty of space between the jars. Check all the lids when cool, tightening as needed. If any of the jars did not seal, refrigerate or freeze instead.

Broccoli Cauliflower Leek Soup

Preserve this healthy vegetable soup as a filling and vitamin-packed meal for when you need it. Serve this dish with a sprinkling of your favorite cheese on top.

Sustainable Storage:
Lasts up to 1 year when canned or 4–6 months in the freezer.

Makes: 6–8 quarts

Ingredients

3 large leeks, trimmed and sliced

8 ounces mushrooms, sliced

1 tablespoon extra-virgin olive oil

6 medium russet potatoes, peeled and cubed

1 head broccoli, trimmed and chopped

1 head cauliflower, trimmed and chopped

1 cup diced onion

6 medium carrots, peeled and diced

2 medium cloves garlic, peeled and minced

1 tablespoon dried basil

⅛ teaspoon salt

⅛ teaspoon freshly ground black pepper

4 quarts chicken broth

1. In a large skillet over medium heat, sauté the leeks and mushrooms in olive oil. Keep leeks separate from mushrooms in skillet.

2. In a large stockpot over medium heat, combine all remaining ingredients. Bring to a full boil.

3. Meanwhile, use a food processor or blender to purée half the leeks. Add puréed leeks, sliced leeks, and mushrooms to boiling soup.

4. Reduce heat to low and simmer another 15 minutes, stirring constantly. If freezing, cool and transfer into freezer-safe containers, leaving ¼" headspace for expansion.

5. If canning, ladle into sterilized jars, leaving 1" headspace at the top of each jar. Make sure to remove all air bubbles. Wipe rims and place sterilized lid on each jar. Tightly screw on sterilized screw bands, and process at 10 pounds of pressure in a pressure canner for 75 minutes for pints or 90 minutes for quarts.

6. Move the jars to a cooling surface, leaving plenty of space between the jars. Check all the lids when cool, tightening as needed. If any of the jars did not seal, refrigerate or freeze instead.

Sweet Potato Ham Soup

Make a large supply of this recipe and experiment with small batches while reheating. This recipe tastes great if you add a pinch of brown sugar and ginger to bring out the sweet potatoes. Alternatively, add a little cornstarch and milk when warming for a scalloped-potato-and-ham-type base.

Sustainable Storage:
Lasts up to 1 year when canned or 4–6 months in the freezer.

Makes: about 2 quarts

Ingredients

4 large sweet potatoes, peeled and cubed

2 pounds ham steak, diced

4 cups ham broth

1 cup water

$\frac{1}{8}$ teaspoon salt

$\frac{1}{8}$ teaspoon freshly ground black pepper

1. In a large stockpot over high heat, combine all ingredients. Bring to a full boil; reduce heat to low and simmer until water has reduced and potatoes are fork-tender. If you are canning, stop cooking before potatoes are tender; they need more firmness for the pressure canner. They should be slightly firmer than those used in potato salad, but time will vary based on size.

2. If freezing, cool and transfer into freezer-safe containers, leaving $\frac{1}{4}$" headspace for expansion. If canning, ladle into sterilized jars, leaving 1" headspace at the top of each jar. Make sure to remove all air bubbles. Wipe rims and place sterilized lid on each jar. Tightly screw on sterilized screw bands, and process at 11 pounds of pressure in a pressure canner for 90 minutes for quarts.

3. Move the jars to a cooling surface, leaving plenty of space between the jars. Check all the lids when cool, tightening as needed. If any of the jars did not seal, refrigerate or freeze instead.

Beef Barley Bliss

If you are canning this recipe, omit the pearl barley and add it when you rewarm the soup for serving.

Sustainable Storage:
Lasts up to 1 year when canned or 4–6 months in the freezer.

Makes: 11–12 quarts

Ingredients

2 cups pearl barley

1 (3-pound) boneless rump roast, diced

3 tablespoons extra-virgin olive oil

7 quarts water

4 medium onions, peeled and chopped

15 large carrots, peeled and diced

8 medium stalks celery, trimmed and chopped

9 medium cloves garlic, peeled and chopped

3 dried bay leaves

1 tablespoon dried tarragon

2 tablespoons dried oregano

2 tablespoons salt

1 tablespoon freshly ground black pepper

1. If freezing soup, prepare barley according to package instructions.

2. In a large stockpot over medium heat, brown beef in olive oil. Scrape the bottom to loosen the little pieces.

3. Raise heat to high and add prepared barley (if freezing) along with remaining ingredients to the stockpot. Bring to a boil, then reduce heat to low and simmer for 1 hour. Taste and adjust seasonings.

4. If freezing, cool and transfer into freezer-safe containers, leaving $\frac{1}{4}$" headspace for expansion. If canning, ladle into sterilized jars, leaving 1" headspace at the top of each jar. Make sure to remove all air bubbles. Wipe rims and place sterilized lid on each jar. Tightly screw on sterilized screw bands, and process at 10 pounds of pressure in a pressure canner for 60 minutes for pints or 75 minutes for quarts.

5. Move the jars to a cooling surface, leaving plenty of space between the jars. Check all the lids when cool, tightening as needed. If any of the jars did not seal, refrigerate or freeze instead.

Veal Stew

This simple and sustainable recipe tastes great with a thick slice of buttered French bread with parsley.

Sustainable Storage:
Lasts up to 1 year when canned or 4–6 months in the freezer.

Makes: 2 quarts

Ingredients

3 pounds veal, cut into
    1" cubes

$\frac{1}{4}$ cup all-purpose flour

3 medium onions, peeled and
    thickly sliced

$\frac{1}{4}$ cup extra-virgin olive oil

2 cups port wine

1 teaspoon salt

1 teaspoon freshly ground
    black pepper

1. In a large bowl, dust diced veal lightly with flour. In a large skillet over medium heat, sauté veal and onions in olive oil.

2. In a large stockpot over low heat, combine veal, onions, and remaining ingredients. Simmer for 3 hours. If you need more liquid, add more wine.

3. If freezing, cool and transfer into freezer-safe containers, leaving $\frac{1}{4}$" headspace for expansion. If canning, ladle into sterilized jars, leaving 1" headspace at the top of each jar. Make sure to remove all air bubbles. Wipe rims and place sterilized lid on each jar. Tightly screw on sterilized screw bands, and process at 10 pounds of pressure in a pressure canner for 75 minutes for pints or 90 minutes for quarts.

4. Move the jars to a cooling surface, leaving plenty of space between the jars. Check all the lids when cool, tightening as needed. If any of the jars did not seal, refrigerate or freeze instead.

Beef Burgundy

You may want to preserve a large supply of this soup for when it becomes a family favorite.

Sustainable Storage:
Lasts up to 1 year when canned or 4–6 months in the freezer.

Makes: 8 quarts

Ingredients

5 pounds roast beef, trimmed and diced into 1" cubes

1 medium beef bone with marrow

1 tablespoon extra-virgin olive oil

5 medium onions, peeled and chopped

15 small shallots, peeled

2 medium cloves garlic, peeled and crushed

6 slices thick bacon, cooked, drained, and crumbled

3 cups diced carrots

2 teaspoons salt

1 teaspoon freshly ground black pepper

3 cups beef broth

10 mushrooms, halved

3 cups Burgundy wine

1. In a large stockpot over medium heat, brown meat and marrow bone in olive oil for 10 minutes.

2. Add onions and continue cooking for 10 more minutes.

3. Add remaining ingredients. Bring to a boil, then reduce heat to low and simmer for 3 hours; remove marrow bone.

4. Cool and skim off excess fat. If freezing, transfer into freezer-safe containers, leaving $\frac{1}{4}$" headspace for expansion. If canning, reheat after skimming off fat. Ladle into sterilized jars, leaving 1" headspace at the top of each jar. Make sure to remove all air bubbles. Wipe rims and place sterilized lid on each jar. Tightly screw on sterilized screw bands, and process at 10 pounds of pressure in a pressure canner for 75 minutes for pints and 90 minutes for quarts.

5. Move the jars to a cooling surface, leaving plenty of space between the jars. Check all the lids when cool, tightening as needed. If any of the jars did not seal, refrigerate or freeze instead.

Black Turtle Bean Soup

Add 2 pints previously cooked and/or home-canned black turtle beans to the puréed mixture for extra flavor.

Sustainable Storage:
Lasts up to 1 year when canned or 4–6 months in the freezer.

Makes: 6 quarts

Ingredients

2 pounds dried black turtle beans

2 ham hocks or ½ pound salt pork

1 cup chopped onion

1 cup chopped celery

1 cup chopped carrots

1 large green bell pepper, seeded and chopped

4 cups peeled and chopped tomatoes with juice

2 tablespoons minced garlic

2–3 beef, vegetable, or chicken bouillon cubes, crushed

2–3 dried bay leaves

½ teaspoon dried basil

½ teaspoon dried oregano

½ teaspoon dried thyme

½ teaspoon chili powder or crushed red pepper flakes, or 1 teaspoon Tabasco sauce

½ teaspoon dried cilantro

⅛ teaspoon salt

⅛ teaspoon freshly ground black pepper

Continued on next page

1. In a large bowl, cover beans with cold water and soak 12–18 hours in a cool place. Drain.

2. Place beans in a large stockpot over high heat and cover with 2" water. Add remaining ingredients and bring to a boil. Reduce heat to low, cover, and simmer for 90 minutes, until beans are tender.

3. Remove and discard bay leaves. Remove meat and chop into small pieces.

4. Press remaining ingredients through a sieve or food mill, or purée in a food processor or blender. Return purée to the stockpot and add meat. If necessary, add boiling water to reach desired consistency. Adjust seasonings to taste.

5. If freezing, cool and transfer into freezer-safe containers, leaving $\frac{1}{4}$" headspace for expansion. If canning, ladle hot soup into sterilized jars, leaving 1" headspace at the top of each jar. Make sure to remove all air bubbles. Wipe rims and place sterilized lid on each jar. Tightly screw on sterilized screw bands, and process at 10 pounds of pressure in a pressure canner for 75 minutes for pints and 90 minutes for quarts.

6. Move the jars to a cooling surface, leaving plenty of space between the jars. Check all the lids when cool, tightening as needed. If any of the jars did not seal, refrigerate or freeze.

Taco Soup

Use your own store of canned diced tomatoes and chili peppers for an extra step in sustainability. Serve this with tortilla chips, shredded cheese, and a teaspoon of sour cream.

Sustainable Storage:
Lasts up to 1 year when canned or 4–6 months in the freezer.

Makes: about 3 quarts

Ingredients

1 ½ pounds lean ground turkey

3 tablespoons extra-virgin olive oil

1 (14-ounce) can diced tomatoes with juice

1 (4-ounce) can diced green chilies, drained

2 (15-ounce) cans kidney beans, drained and rinsed

1 medium onion, peeled and diced

1 teaspoon diced garlic

4 cups water or chicken broth

1 (1.25-ounce) package taco seasoning mix

1. In a large skillet over medium heat, brown turkey with olive oil. Drain off excess fat. In a large stockpot over low heat, combine cooked turkey and all remaining ingredients. Simmer for 45–60 minutes.

2. If freezing, cool and transfer into freezer-safe containers, leaving ¼" headspace for expansion. If canning, ladle hot soup into sterilized wide-mouth quart jars, leaving 1" headspace at the top of each jar. Make sure to remove all air bubbles. Wipe rims and place sterilized lid on each jar. Tightly screw on sterilized screw bands, and process at 10 pounds of pressure in a pressure canner for 65 minutes.

3. Move the jars to a cooling surface, leaving plenty of space between the jars. Check all the lids when cool, tightening as needed. If any of the jars did not seal, refrigerate or freeze instead.

Poor Man's Minestrone

This sustainable recipe can use your stored leftover vegetable ends and pieces. Tie them in cheesecloth and let them soak in the soup.

Sustainable Storage:
Lasts up to 1 year when canned or 4–6 months in the freezer.

Makes: 3–4 quarts

Ingredients

1 pound lean ground beef

1 large onion, peeled and chopped

1 medium clove garlic, peeled and minced

2 tablespoons extra-virgin olive oil

1 (16–ounce) can low-fat beef broth

9 cups water

1 (6-ounce) can tomato paste

1 (16-ounce) can kidney beans, drained

1 cup sliced celery

1 cup sliced carrots

$\frac{1}{2}$ teaspoon salt

$\frac{1}{8}$ teaspoon freshly ground black pepper

$\frac{1}{4}$ teaspoon dried oregano

1 cup chopped cabbage

1 cup frozen peas

1 large zucchini, trimmed and sliced

1. In a large skillet over medium heat, brown ground beef, onion, and garlic with olive oil; drain off fat. In a large stockpot over high heat, combine the ground beef mixture with remaining ingredients. Bring to a boil. Cover and reduce heat; simmer for 10 minutes.

2. If freezing, cool and transfer into freezer-safe containers, leaving $\frac{1}{4}$" headspace for expansion. If canning, ladle hot soup into sterilized jars, leaving 1" headspace at the top of each jar. Make sure to remove all air bubbles. Wipe rims and place sterilized lid on each jar. Tightly screw on sterilized screw bands, and process at 10 pounds of pressure in a pressure canner for 75 minutes for pints or 90 minutes for quarts.

3. Move the jars to a cooling surface, leaving plenty of space between the jars. Check all the lids when cool, tightening as needed. If any of the jars did not seal, refrigerate or freeze instead.

Preservation Pointers

To safely can ground meat, after cooking and layering in jars while hot, the meat should be drained and covered with a matching broth, leaving 1" headspace.

Dried Vegetable Soup Mix

This recipe can be made in bulk and put into food-storage bags. While it takes time to dry the vegetables, the resulting product saves a lot of shelf space.

Sustainable Storage:
Lasts up to 1 year.

Makes: 4 cups

Ingredients

2 medium stalks celery, trimmed and chopped

2 medium carrots, peeled and chopped

1 cup diced broccoli

1 cup diced cauliflower

1 cup diced cabbage

1 cup thinly sliced potatoes

1 cup diced onion

1 cup diced mixed bell peppers

1 cup quartered cherry tomatoes

½ cup diced leeks

1 cup fresh peas

1 cup powdered vegetable soup broth

1. Place each vegetable on a separate tray of your dehydrator. Set dehydrator to appropriate temperature as specified by the manufacturer. If you are drying vegetables in the oven, dry each type of vegetable separately, because some will dry faster than others. Bake at 150°F. On average, vegetables take 6–12 hours to dry completely to a crunchy texture. Carrots and onions take 3–6 hours; celery takes 6–8 hours; broccoli takes 6–14 hours; bell peppers take 4–6 hours; and potatoes, peas, and cabbage take 8–11 hours.

2. In a large bowl, mix all dried vegetables together with soup broth. Store in a cool, dry area for use in flavoring soup or stews or as instant soup mix.

Pickled Soup

This Pickled Soup made with your own preserved soup broth is the pinnacle of self-sustainability. If you like, thicken this recipe just before serving with an egg and flour roux. Top with 1 tablespoon sour cream.

Sustainable Storage:
Lasts up to 1 year when canned or 4–6 months in the freezer.

Makes: 12 cups

Ingredients

8 cups Dill Pickle Soup Broth (see recipe in this chapter)

2 chicken bouillon cubes

2 medium carrots, peeled and coarsely grated

2 cups cubed potatoes

1 cup thinly sliced celery

5 large dill pickles, grated

$\frac{1}{8}$ teaspoon salt

$\frac{1}{8}$ teaspoon freshly ground black pepper

1. In a large pot over high heat, combine broth, bouillon cubes, carrots, potatoes, and celery. Cook until potatoes are tender, about 10 minutes.

2. Add pickles. Continue cooking about 15 minutes more.

3. Taste, adding salt and pepper if desired. If freezing, cool and transfer into freezer-safe containers, leaving $\frac{1}{4}$" headspace for expansion. If canning, ladle hot soup into sterilized jars, leaving 1" headspace at the top of each jar. Make sure to remove all air bubbles. Wipe rims and place sterilized lid on each jar. Tightly screw on sterilized screw bands, and process at 10 pounds of pressure in a pressure canner for 75 minutes.

4. Move the jars to a cooling surface, leaving plenty of space between the jars. Check all the lids when cool, tightening as needed. If any of the jars did not seal, refrigerate or freeze instead.

Sweet Pickle Stew

This sustainable stew is complete with your favorite homemade sweet pickles to top off the flavor.

Sustainable Storage:
Lasts up to 1 year when canned or 4–6 months in the freezer.

Makes: 2 quarts

Ingredients

2 pounds ground beef or turkey

4 tablespoons extra-virgin olive oil

$\frac{1}{2}$ cup peeled and diced potato

$\frac{1}{2}$ cup diced onion

$\frac{1}{2}$ cup peeled and diced carrot

1 (16–ounce) can tomato sauce

1 cup water

$\frac{1}{2}$ cup diced sweet pickles

$\frac{1}{2}$ cup pickle juice or wine

$\frac{1}{8}$ teaspoon salt

$\frac{1}{8}$ teaspoon freshly ground black pepper

1. In a large skillet over medium heat, cook the ground meat in olive oil until browned. Drain off fat. Transfer cooked meat to a slow cooker. Add remaining ingredients and cook on low for 6 hours.

2. If freezing, cool and transfer into freezer-safe containers, leaving $\frac{1}{4}$" headspace for expansion. If canning, ladle hot soup into sterilized jars, leaving 1" headspace at the top of each jar. Make sure to remove all air bubbles. Wipe rims and place sterilized lid on each jar. Tightly screw on sterilized screw bands, and process at 10 pounds of pressure in a pressure canner for 75 minutes for pints and 90 minutes for quarts.

3. Move the jars to a cooling surface, leaving plenty of space between the jars. Check all the lids when cool, tightening as needed. If any of the jars did not seal, refrigerate or freeze instead.

Preservation Pointers

The stews in this cookbook are not as thick as traditional stews. This allows them to be canned safely. You can freeze thicker stews, but you may find the gravy is a little lumpy upon warming.

CHAPTER NINE

Vegetables

Green Tomato Raspberry Jam

You can use whatever type of gelatin you like in this. No one will ever know there are homegrown tomatoes in it!

Sustainable Storage:
Lasts up to 2 years when canned or 1 year in the freezer.

Makes: 8–9 pints

Ingredients

8 cups grated green tomatoes

1/2 cup fresh lemon juice

2 teaspoons orange extract

3 tablespoons dried orange zest

8 cups granulated sugar

2 (6-ounce) packages
raspberry-flavored gelatin mix

1. In a large saucepan over medium heat, combine tomatoes, lemon juice, orange extract, orange zest, and sugar. Bring to a boil. Stir and cook for about 10 minutes.

2. Add gelatin mix. Reduce heat to low and simmer for 20 minutes.

3. If freezing, cool and transfer into freezer-safe containers, leaving 1/4" headspace for expansion.

4. If canning, pour into sterilized jars, leaving 1/4" headspace at the top of each jar. Make sure to remove all air bubbles. Wipe rims and place sterilized lid on each jar. Tightly screw on sterilized screw bands, and process in a water-bath canner for 10 minutes.

5. Move the jars to a cooling surface, leaving plenty of space between the jars. Check all the lids when cool, tightening as needed. If any of the jars did not seal, refrigerate or freeze instead.

Corn Relish

Your sustainable preserved food doesn't have to be boring! This is a bright, beautiful dish, in terms of both appearance and flavor. Try it served with crab cakes.

Sustainable Storage:
Lasts up to 1 year.

Makes: 5–6 pints

Ingredients

10 cups uncooked sweet baby corn kernels

1 cup diced red bell pepper

1 cup diced green bell pepper

1 cup diced celery

$\frac{1}{2}$ cup sliced red onion

$\frac{1}{2}$ cup diced Vidalia onion

$1\frac{1}{2}$ cups granulated sugar

$2\frac{1}{2}$ cups white vinegar

2 cups water

1 teaspoon salt

2 teaspoons celery seeds

2 teaspoons whole yellow mustard seeds

1. In a large pot over medium heat, combine all ingredients. Bring to a fast boil; reduce heat and simmer for 15 minutes.

2. Pack hot relish into sterilized jars, leaving $\frac{1}{2}$" headspace at the top of each jar. Make sure to remove all air bubbles. Wipe rims and place sterilized lid on each jar. Tightly screw on sterilized screw bands, and process in a water-bath canner for 15 minutes.

3. Move the jars to a cooling surface, leaving plenty of space between the jars. Check all the lids when cool, tightening as needed. If any of the jars did not seal, refrigerate or freeze instead.

Sauerkraut

This recipe is based on a traditional method of making kraut in a brine crock. Passed down through generations, this Sauerkraut is both delicious and sustainable. You'll need a large 3-gallon crock.

Sustainable Storage:
Lasts up to 1 year.

Makes: 4 quarts

Ingredients

12 pounds cabbage, cored and shredded into $1/4$" pieces

$3/4$ cup pickling salt

1. Mix cabbage with salt; pack firmly into brine crock, fill crock, leaving 5" headspace. If the brine released from the cabbage does not cover the cabbage, boil some water, cool it, and then add it to the crock until the cabbage is completely covered.

2. Use a small bowl, plate, or other weight on top to keep cabbage down submerged; cover crock with an airtight lid.

3. Leave cabbage 5 weeks to ferment (75°F is the best temperature).

4. Move sauerkraut to a nonaluminum pot on low heat; simmer until heated through.

5. Pack hot sauerkraut into sterilized quart jars, leaving $1/2$" headspace at the top of each jar. Make sure to remove all air bubbles. Wipe rims and place sterilized lid on each jar. Tightly screw on sterilized screw bands, and process in a water-bath canner for 20 minutes for quarts.

6. Move the jars to a cooling surface, leaving plenty of space between the jars. Check all the lids when cool, tightening as needed. If any of the jars did not seal, refrigerate or freeze instead.

Spiced Artichoke Hearts

Preserve and use these Spiced Artichoke Hearts for anything—as appetizers, a topping to green salad, or with pasta salad. The flavor improves if served with a little extra-virgin olive oil.

Sustainable Storage:
Lasts up to 1 year.

Makes: 4½ pints

Ingredients

2½ cups frozen artichoke hearts, defrosted and blanched

¼ cup white wine vinegar

¼ cup red wine vinegar

½ cup water

4 medium cloves garlic, peeled

¼ teaspoon dried thyme

¼ teaspoon dried parsley

¼ teaspoon dried rosemary

½ teaspoon dried basil

½ teaspoon dried oregano

⅛ teaspoon crushed red pepper flakes

1. Divide artichokes among four (half-pint) sterilized jars.

2. In a small saucepan over high heat, mix together remaining ingredients; heat to boiling.

3. Pour into jars over artichokes, leaving ½" headspace at the top of each jar. Make sure to remove all air bubbles. Wipe rims and place sterilized lid on each jar. Tightly screw on sterilized screw bands, and process in a water-bath canner for 15 minutes.

4. Move the jars to a cooling surface, leaving plenty of space between the jars. Check all the lids when cool, tightening as needed. If any of the jars did not seal, refrigerate or freeze instead.

Jumpin' Vegetable Juice

Skip the overprocessed store-bought vegetable juice and preserve this healthy beverage instead. It can be canned or frozen.

Sustainable Storage: Lasts up to 1 year.

Makes: about 6 quarts

Ingredients

15 pounds ripe tomatoes, cored and chopped

1 small yellow, orange, or red bell pepper, seeded and chopped

1 small green bell pepper, seeded and chopped

1 cup diced celery

2 medium carrots, diced

2 dried bay leaves

2 teaspoons dried basil

1 tablespoon salt

1 tablespoon freshly ground horseradish

$\frac{1}{2}$ teaspoon freshly ground black pepper

1 teaspoon granulated sugar

2 teaspoons Worcestershire sauce

1. In a large, nonreactive pot over low heat, combine all ingredients. Simmer for 45 minutes, stirring periodically.

2. Put entire mixture through a sieve or juicer to remove any fibers, skins, and seeds. Repeat to achieve a fine consistency.

3. Return mixture to pot over high heat; bring to a boil. Pack into sterilized quart jars, leaving $\frac{1}{2}$" headspace at the top of each jar. Make sure to remove all air bubbles. Wipe rims and place sterilized lid on each jar. Tightly screw on sterilized screw bands, and process in a water-bath canner for 30 minutes.

4. Move the jars to a cooling surface, leaving plenty of space between the jars. Check all the lids when cool, tightening as needed. If any of the jars did not seal, refrigerate or freeze instead.

Candied Sweet Potatoes

These are great to have on hand when you need a side dish for turkey or chicken. The vanilla extract and pumpkin pie spice add just the right kick.

Sustainable Storage:
Lasts up to 1 year.

Makes: 4 quarts

Ingredients

12 pounds sweet potatoes

5 medium oranges

1 1/2 cups firmly packed light brown sugar

1 cup honey

2 tablespoons pure vanilla extract

1 1/2 tablespoons pumpkin pie spice

1. In a large pot over medium heat, boil potatoes in enough water to cover until skins come off easily, about 20 minutes.

2. While potatoes cook, prepare orange sauce. Grate 1/4 cup zest and set aside. Juice oranges and add enough water to make 2 1/2 cups. In a medium saucepan over medium-high heat, combine orange juice mixture, brown sugar, and honey. Bring to a boil, stirring constantly until brown sugar dissolves. Stir in vanilla, orange zest, and pumpkin pie spice. Cover and keep hot.

3. Immerse cooked potatoes in cold water. Rub and pull skins off. Cut potatoes into chunks.

4. Pack potatoes into sterilized jars, leaving 1" headspace at the top of each jar. Ladle 1/3 cup hot syrup into pint jars (3/4 cup syrup for quarts). Make sure to remove all air bubbles. Wipe rims and place sterilized lid on each jar. Tightly screw on sterilized screw bands, and process at 10 pounds of pressure in a pressure canner for 65 minutes for pints or 90 minutes for quarts.

5. Move the jars to a cooling surface, leaving plenty of space between the jars. Check all the lids when cool, tightening as needed. If any of the jars did not seal, refrigerate or freeze instead.

Herbed Corn on the Cob

Make these at the fall harvest and warm them up on a cold winter day for a lasting taste of summer picnics.

Sustainable Storage:
Lasts up to 9 months.

Makes: 12 ears

Ingredients

8 tablespoons unsalted butter, softened

1 teaspoon salt

1 teaspoon freshly ground black pepper

1 teaspoon dried parsley

½ teaspoon garlic powder

½ teaspoon onion powder

¼ teaspoon chipotle powder

12 ears corn, husked and blanched

1. In a small bowl, mix all ingredients except corn until evenly incorporated. Spread the herbed butter evenly over each ear of corn. Wrap ears tightly with plastic wrap, twisting top and bottom of wrap.

2. Wrap in a layer of aluminum foil. Place in a large resealable food-storage bag and freeze.

3. When ready to use, take out of food-storage bag and defrost. Ears can be grilled or broiled in oven for 15–20 minutes. (The plastic will not melt inside the foil.)

Baked Stuffed Potatoes

Make and preserve these simple Baked Stuffed Potatoes for a warm and filling snack or side dish when you want it.

Sustainable Storage:
Lasts 6–8 months.

Makes: 6 stuffed potatoes

Ingredients

6 large Idaho potatoes, baked

4 tablespoons salted butter, softened

½ cup diced green onions

¼ cup crumbled bacon bits

1 cup shredded sharp Cheddar cheese

1. Scoop out insides of potatoes, leaving enough to make a good shell for freezing and baking. Place potato insides in a large bowl.

2. Mash potatoes with butter, green onions, bacon bits, and cheese. Refill potato skins, then wrap individually using freezer-safe wrap. Double wrap to avoid freezer burn and label accordingly.

3. To reheat, thaw potatoes. Preheat the oven to 400°F. Remove plastic from potatoes and bake for 30 minutes, until cheese is fully melted.

Stuffed Shiitake Mushrooms

Preserve these Stuffed Shiitake Mushrooms in bulk ahead of time. When you're ready to enjoy, defrost them, preheat the oven to 400°F, and put the mushrooms on a baking sheet with a slice of mozzarella cheese on top. They'll be ready in about 15 minutes!

Sustainable Storage:
Lasts up to 4 months.

Makes: 6 stuffed mushrooms

Ingredients

2 tablespoons chopped onion

2 tablespoons chopped celery

1 tablespoon minced garlic

3 tablespoons unsalted butter

1 teaspoon fresh lemon juice

1 cup finely diced cooked crabmeat

$\frac{1}{2}$ cup herbed bread crumbs

$\frac{1}{4}$ cup dry white wine

6 (4"–5"–diameter) shiitake mushrooms, blanched for 2 minutes

$\frac{1}{2}$ tablespoon extra-virgin olive oil

$\frac{1}{8}$ teaspoon salt

$\frac{1}{8}$ teaspoon freshly ground black pepper

1. In a medium skillet over medium heat, combine onion, celery, garlic, butter, and lemon juice. Sauté until vegetables are soft. Transfer to a medium mixing bowl. Add crabmeat, bread crumbs, and white wine. Mix completely.

2. Brush mushroom caps with olive oil and sprinkle all sides with salt and pepper.

3. Divide the crab mixture evenly among mushroom caps. Wrap carefully with freezer-safe wrap.

Honey Almond Carrots

You'll thank yourself later for preserving this delightful side dish. The orange juice and peel marry perfectly with the sweetness of the carrots.

Sustainable Storage:
Lasts up to 1 year.

Makes: 3 quarts

Ingredients

8 pounds carrots, peeled
    and sliced

6 cups water

3 cups orange juice

³⁄₄ cup honey

2 tablespoons vanilla extract

¹⁄₂ cup orange peel

¹⁄₃ cup sliced almonds

1 tablespoon crystallized ginger

1. Boil carrots until they are tender but not mushy. Drain and set aside.

2. In a large saucepan over medium heat, prepare syrup by combining water, orange juice, and honey. Bring to a boil, then reduce heat to low and simmer for 10 minutes until syrup starts to thicken slightly. Remove from heat and stir in vanilla. Pack cooked carrots into sterilized jars.

3. Divide orange peel, sliced almonds, and crystallized ginger evenly among jars. Pour hot syrup over carrots, leaving 1" headspace at the top of each jar. Make sure to remove all air bubbles. Wipe rims and place sterilized lid on each jar. Tightly screw on sterilized screw bands, and process at 10 pounds of pressure in a pressure canner for 30 minutes for quarts.

Stuffed Blackened Bell Peppers

Preserve these Stuffed Blackened Bell Peppers for a healthy and natural source of vitamins A and C and antioxidants that bolster the immune system.

Sustainable Storage:
Lasts up to 4 months.

Makes: 12 appetizers

Ingredients

6 large bell peppers

1 1/2 tablespoons extra-virgin olive oil, divided

2 teaspoons salt

1/4 teaspoon freshly ground black pepper

1 tablespoon unsalted butter

1/2 cup chopped onion

1/2 cup chopped celery

1 medium clove garlic, peeled and crushed

1 cup tomato sauce

1 teaspoon Worcestershire sauce

1 teaspoon dried oregano

1/2 teaspoon dried basil

1 1/2 pounds lean ground beef, cooked and drained of fat

3/4 cup shredded cheddar cheese

1. Preheat broiler to high. Place peppers in oven. When skins are bubbly and black, remove and cool.

2. Remove blackened skins. Halve each pepper and remove seeds; brush lightly with 1/2 tablespoon olive oil and sprinkle with salt and pepper. Set aside.

3. In a large skillet over medium heat, heat remaining 1 tablespoon olive oil and butter; add onion, celery, and garlic. Cook until vegetables are soft, then add tomato sauce, Worcestershire sauce, oregano, and basil. Reduce heat to low and simmer for 15 minutes.

4. Stir in cooked ground beef; remove from heat and cool.

5. Stir in cheese. Divide mixture evenly among pepper halves.

6. Wrap carefully in freezer-safe wrap.

Vegetable Lover's Lasagna

This is a great recipe for putting your blanched garden vegetables to use! You can certainly add meat if you wish, but this dish is very rich without. Note that you can simply freeze large slabs of this lasagna rather than single servings if you prefer.

Sustainable Storage: Lasts 2–3 months.

Makes: 12 servings

Ingredients

20 ounces mixed vegetables, chopped and blanched

1 medium red onion, peeled and sliced

3 medium cloves garlic, peeled and minced

2 tablespoons chopped fresh basil

1 tablespoon extra-virgin olive oil

2 teaspoons Italian seasoning

1 (12-ounce) container ricotta cheese

2 large eggs, beaten

5 cups mixed shredded Italian cheeses, such as Parmesan, Asiago, etc.

1 (16-ounce) can tomato or spaghetti sauce

1 (12-ounce) package lasagna noodles, cooked

3 cups prepared Alfredo sauce

1. Cook mixed vegetables by your preferred method until tender; set aside.

2. In a medium skillet over medium heat, sauté onion, garlic, and basil in olive oil. Remove from heat.

3. In a large bowl, combine cooked vegetables with onion mixture, tossing to coat evenly.

4. In a separate large bowl, combine Italian seasoning, ricotta, eggs, and Italian cheeses.

5. Line a 9" × 13" pan with aluminum foil. Cover with a layer of tomato sauce. Lay down one layer of noodles, followed by vegetables, ricotta mixture, and Alfredo sauce. Repeat the layering until you fill the pan.

6. Cover and place in the freezer until it's solid enough to cut into twelve pieces.

7. Slice and double-wrap each piece in plastic wrap and aluminum foil and put into a freezer-safe food-storage bag for single servings.

8. To warm, preheat the oven to 350°F. Remove lasagna from the wrappings and place in an ovenproof pan. Cover with aluminum foil and bake for about 30 minutes for a single piece. Uncover and bake another 10 minutes to finish.

Vegetable Medley

This dish is braised in the oven before being moved and preserved in single-serving aluminum foil containers—perfect for camping trips or any day you need a sustainable side dish.

Sustainable Storage:
Lasts up to 6 months.

Makes: about 10 servings

Ingredients

1 pound baby carrots, peeled

1 pound young parsnips, peeled and halved

1 pound fingerling potatoes, halved

1 medium red onion, peeled and sliced

10 medium stalks celery, trimmed and cut in 1" pieces

1 (12-ounce) container cherry tomatoes

10 teaspoons prepared vinaigrette, divided

2 teaspoons chopped garlic, divided

$\frac{1}{8}$ teaspoon salt, divided

$\frac{1}{8}$ teaspoon freshly ground black pepper, divided

10 sprigs fresh rosemary, divided

1. Preheat the oven to 400°F. Oil a large roasting tray and set aside.

2. In a large bowl, toss carrots, parsnips, potatoes, onion, celery, and tomatoes with 5 teaspoons vinaigrette, coating them evenly.

3. Transfer vegetables to the prepared tray and roast for 20 minutes, stirring regularly. They will not be completely tender.

4. Set out ten pieces of aluminum foil about 12"–14" long. Put equal portions of the vegetable blend on each piece of foil.

5. Add $\frac{1}{2}$ teaspoon of remaining vinaigrette to each package. Distribute garlic, salt, and pepper evenly among the packages, and lay a sprig of rosemary on top of each. Wrap the vegetables into an envelope-style bundle and wrap with a second layer of aluminum foil, and freeze.

6. To cook, defrost. Preheat the oven to 400°F. Roast vegetables in the oven or on the grill for 20 minutes.

Dried Hot Pepper Flakes

This is a good way to use up those leftovers from the garden. It also provides an excuse for a trip to the farmers' market! It doesn't matter how many varieties you mix together.

Sustainable Storage:
Lasts up to 3 years.

Makes: 1 cup

Ingredients

5 cups ¼" pieces chopped hot peppers (any variety)

1. Preheat oven to 200°F. Line a baking sheet with heavy-duty aluminum foil; lightly spray with cooking spray. Evenly spread chopped peppers onto baking sheet.

2. Place in oven, leaving oven door slightly ajar. Bake 3–4 hours, turning with a long-handled spatula every 30 minutes. Peppers should be bone dry.

3. Leave on kitchen counter for a few days to make sure flakes crumble when picked up. Store in a Mason jar with a tight-fitting cover. Label clearly.

Vegetable Chips

This makes a healthy and sustainable snack that has a long shelf life and can also double as the base for a vegetable soup or stew.

Sustainable Storage:
Lasts up to 5 years.

Makes: about 10 cups

Ingredients

2 large potatoes, thinly sliced and blanched for 1 minute

1 medium sweet potato, peeled and thinly sliced and blanched for 1 minute

3 large radishes, peeled and thinly sliced and blanched for 1 minute

2 large carrots, peeled and thinly sliced and blanched for 1 minute

2 large parsnips, peeled and thinly sliced and blanched for 1 minute

2 tablespoons extra-virgin olive oil

½ teaspoon salt

1 teaspoon garlic powder

1. In a large bowl, toss vegetables with olive oil, salt, garlic powder, and any other spices you like.

2. Sort in layers by vegetable type and transfer to a dehydrator, using the temperature setting recommended by the manufacturer. Dry about 6 hours, until crispy.

3. Store in airtight container.

Traditional Dilly Beans

These are a seasonal favorite that can be preserved and enjoyed year-round. For a change of tastes, try using these pickles as the base for a green bean casserole.

Sustainable Storage: Lasts up to 1 year.

Makes: 4 pints

Ingredients

2 pounds fresh green beans, trimmed and blanched

8 sprigs fresh dill

4 medium cloves garlic, peeled

2 cups white vinegar

½ cup red wine vinegar

4 teaspoons canning and pickling salt

2½ cups water

1. If necessary, cut beans to fit canning jars. Pack beans into sterilized jars. Place 2 sprigs dill and 1 clove garlic in each jar.

2. In a medium saucepan over high heat, combine white vinegar, red wine vinegar, salt, and water; bring to a boil. Remove from heat.

3. Pour over the beans, leaving ½" headspace at the top of each jar. Make sure to remove all air bubbles. Wipe rims and place sterilized lid on each jar. Tightly screw on sterilized screw bands, and process in a water-bath canner for 10 minutes.

4. Move the jars to a cooling surface, leaving plenty of space between the jars. Check all the lids when cool, tightening as needed. If any of the jars did not seal, refrigerate or freeze instead.

Sweet Minted Eggplant

Preserve and pickle your small garden eggplants with this delicious recipe. These pickles do not need to be chilled for serving. In fact, they're tastiest at room temperature.

Sustainable Storage:
Lasts 3–4 months in the refrigerator.

Makes: about 3 cups

Ingredients

1 pound small eggplants, cut into $\frac{1}{2}$"-thick rounds

1 tablespoon canning and pickling salt

2 tablespoons fresh lemon juice

2 tablespoons white vinegar

2 tablespoons honey

$\frac{1}{2}$ cup extra-virgin olive oil

2 tablespoons minced garlic

$\frac{1}{3}$ cup chopped fresh mint

Zest of 1 medium lemon

$\frac{1}{4}$ teaspoon crushed red pepper flakes

$\frac{1}{8}$ teaspoon salt

$\frac{1}{8}$ teaspoon freshly ground black pepper

1. Sprinkle eggplant slices with pickling salt; let stand 30 minutes.

2. Preheat oven broiler to high. Lightly grease a baking sheet and set aside.

3. In a large bowl, whisk together remaining ingredients; toss eggplant in mixture to coat evenly.

4. Remove eggplant, but reserve the honey and vinegar mixture. Lay eggplant slices on prepared baking sheet. Broil lightly for 3 minutes on each side.

5. Return eggplant to the large bowl and toss again in honey mixture. Pack into small jars and refrigerate.

Preservation Pointers

Eggplant is a member of the nightshade family, so it is related to tomatoes and potatoes. When you shop for eggplants, look for fruits with smooth, firm skin. The skin should give when you press it gently, but it should not be mushy or discolored.

Green Tomato Piccalilli

A sustainable and self-sufficient side dish or condiment. It'll brighten up your hamburgers and hot dogs with its vibrant color.

Sustainable Storage:
Lasts up to 1 year.

Makes: 6–8 pints

Ingredients

16 cups finely chopped green tomatoes

$\frac{1}{2}$ medium head green cabbage, cored and finely chopped

$\frac{1}{2}$ cup canning and pickling salt

4 cups apple cider vinegar

$1\frac{1}{2}$ cups firmly packed dark brown sugar

$\frac{1}{2}$ tablespoon whole yellow mustard seeds

$\frac{1}{2}$ tablespoon ground cinnamon

1 tablespoon freshly ground black pepper

$\frac{1}{8}$ teaspoon crushed red pepper flakes

$\frac{1}{2}$ tablespoon ground allspice

1 tablespoon ground ginger

1 tablespoon dill seeds

1. In a very large bowl or pot, combine vegetables and pickling salt; add enough water to cover, and soak overnight. Drain and rinse vegetables.

2. In a large pot over high heat, combine remaining ingredients. Bring to a boil. Add drained vegetables and return mixture to a boil. Reduce heat to low and simmer until vegetables are tender, about 30 minutes.

3. Pack into sterilized jars, leaving $\frac{1}{4}$" headspace at the top of each jar. Make sure to remove all air bubbles. Wipe rims and place sterilized lid on each jar. Tightly screw on sterilized screw bands, and process in a water-bath canner for 15 minutes.

4. Move the jars to a cooling surface, leaving plenty of space between the jars. Check all the lids when cool, tightening as needed. If any of the jars did not seal, refrigerate or freeze instead.

Gracious Garlic Dills

Nothing goes together quite so well as dill and garlic. These delicious pickles are what preserving for self-sustainability is all about!

Sustainable Storage:
Lasts up to 10 months after 2 months of aging.

Makes: 8 quarts

Ingredients

8 pounds pickling cucumbers

4 cups white vinegar

3 quarts water

$\frac{2}{3}$ cup canning and pickling salt

16 medium cloves garlic, peeled, divided

16 sprigs fresh dill, divided

2 teaspoons minced garlic, divided

2 teaspoons dried dill, divided

1. Soak cucumbers in ice water for 2 hours. If you're planning to slice these, wait until just before canning.

2. In a large pot over high heat, combine vinegar, water, and pickling salt. Bring to a boil.

3. Place 2 cloves garlic, 2 sprigs dill, $\frac{1}{4}$ teaspoon minced garlic, and $\frac{1}{4}$ teaspoon dried dill into each of 8 sterilized quart jars. Pack each jar with approximately 1 pound cucumbers.

4. Fill jars with brine, leaving 1" headspace at the top of each jar. Make sure cucumbers are fully covered. Remove any air bubbles.

5. Wipe rims and place sterilized lid on each jar. Tightly screw on sterilized screw bands, and process in a water-bath canner for 15 minutes.

6. Move the jars to a cooling surface, leaving plenty of space between the jars. Check all the lids when cool, tightening as needed. If any of the jars did not seal, refrigerate or freeze instead. Age for 2 months before eating.

Dad's Freezer Pickles

This recipe is highly adaptable. If you'll be preserving in bulk, make several batches in which you tinker with other spices and add other vegetables for a range of stored blends.

Sustainable Storage:
Lasts up to 1 year when canned or 3–4 months in the freezer.

Makes: 2 quarts

Ingredients

12 cups thinly sliced cucumbers

4 cups thinly sliced sweet onions

3 cups granulated sugar

3 cups white vinegar

1 teaspoon canning and pickling salt

1 teaspoon whole yellow mustard seeds

1 teaspoon celery seeds

1. Place cucumbers and onions in a large nonreactive bowl.

2. In a saucepan over high heat, combine remaining ingredients; bring to a boil. Stir until sugar is dissolved.

3. Pour brine over cucumbers. Put a plate on top of cucumbers so they stay submerged in brine; let sit at room temperature 24 hours.

4. If freezing, transfer into freezer-safe containers, leaving $\frac{1}{4}$" headspace for expansion. If canning, pack vegetables and brine into sterilized jars, leaving $\frac{1}{4}$" headspace at the top of each jar. Make sure to remove all air bubbles. Wipe rims and place sterilized lid on each jar. Tightly screw on sterilized screw bands, and process in a water-bath canner for 15 minutes.

5. Move the jars to a cooling surface, leaving plenty of space between the jars. Check all the lids when cool, tightening as needed. If any of the jars did not seal, refrigerate or freeze instead.

CHAPTER TEN

Fruit

Persimmon Butter

This canning recipe comes together nearly instantaneously.

Sustainable Storage:
Lasts up to 1 year.

Makes: 5–6 pints

Ingredients

8 cups persimmon purée

1 cup orange juice

1½ cups honey

Zest of 1 medium orange

1. In a large stockpot over medium-high heat, combine all ingredients and heat until thickened, about 10–15 minutes.

2. Ladle hot mixture into sterilized jars, leaving ¼" headspace at the top of each jar. Make sure to remove all air bubbles. Wipe rims and place sterilized lid on each jar. Tightly screw on sterilized screw bands, and process in a water-bath canner for 10 minutes.

3. Move the jars to a cooling surface, leaving plenty of space between the jars. Check all the lids when cool, tightening as needed. If any of the jars did not seal, refrigerate or freeze instead.

Berry Bliss

Preserve your fresh foraged berries with this delightful Berry Bliss recipe.

Sustainable Storage:
Lasts up to 1 year.

Makes: 4 pints

Ingredients

4 cups prepared sugar syrup, divided

8 cups mixed fresh berries, bruised spots removed, divided

1. Heat sugar syrup to boiling; fill each jar with ½ cup syrup. Add berries, leaving ½" headspace and making sure berries are covered in liquid. Remove any air bubbles.

2. Wipe rims and place sterilized lid on each jar. Tightly screw on sterilized screw bands, and process in a water-bath canner for 15 minutes.

Preservation Pointers

Many fruit recipes call for a sugar syrup. Make your own by combining granulated sugar and water in a medium saucepan and bringing the mixture to a boil over high heat, stirring to dissolve the sugar. The ratio of sugar to water differs depending on how heavy a syrup is desired.

Lemon Zesty Pears

The pears and lemon combine to make a delicious topper, side dish, or dessert. Go the extra step with your self-sustainability and use the syrup for bastes and marinades. Just be sure to temper with some vinegar or more lemon juice if you do.

Sustainable Storage:
Lasts up to 1 year.

Makes: 3 quarts

Ingredients

8 pounds pears, peeled, cored, and halved or quartered

$\frac{1}{4}$ teaspoon Fruit-Fresh (ascorbic acid)

2 cups granulated sugar

$\frac{3}{8}$ teaspoon freshly grated lemon zest

4 cups water

1. Following package directions, treat pears with Fruit-Fresh to prevent darkening.

2. To make syrup, in a large stockpot, combine sugar, lemon zest, and water; stir well. Heat until boiling; reduce heat to medium. Add pears and cook until tender, 5–6 minutes. Ladle hot pears into sterilized jars, leaving $\frac{1}{2}$" headspace at the top of each jar.

3. Ladle hot syrup over pears, preserving $\frac{1}{2}$" headspace. Make sure to remove all air bubbles. Wipe rims and place sterilized lid on each jar. Tightly screw on sterilized screw bands, and process in a water-bath canner for 20 minutes for pints or 25 minutes for quarts.

4. Move the jars to a cooling surface, leaving plenty of space between the jars. Check all the lids when cool, tightening as needed. If any of the jars did not seal, refrigerate or freeze instead.

Raspberry Salsa

Preserve and store this fruity salsa, which works for snacking and as a topping for meat.

Sustainable Storage:
Lasts up to 1 year.

Makes: $3\frac{1}{2}$ pints

Ingredients

6 cups fresh raspberries, divided

$1\frac{1}{4}$ cups chopped red onions

4 medium jalapeño peppers, seeded and finely chopped

1 large red bell pepper, seeded and chopped

$\frac{3}{4}$ cup finely chopped and loosely packed fresh cilantro

Juice and zest of 2 medium limes

$\frac{1}{2}$ cup white vinegar

4 tablespoons balsamic vinegar

3 tablespoons honey

3 medium cloves garlic, peeled and finely minced

$1\frac{1}{2}$ teaspoons ground cumin

$\frac{1}{2}$ teaspoon ground cayenne pepper

1 teaspoon ground coriander

$\frac{1}{2}$ teaspoon freshly ground black pepper

1. Put half the raspberries in a large stockpot and mash lightly. Add the remaining raspberries and the remaining ingredients. Bring to a boil, stirring constantly to prevent scorching. Boil gently for 5 minutes.

2. Ladle hot salsa into sterilized jars, leaving $\frac{1}{4}$" headspace at the top of each jar. Make sure to remove all air bubbles. Wipe rims and place sterilized lid on each jar. Tightly screw on sterilized screw bands, and process in a water-bath canner for 15 minutes.

3. Move the jars to a cooling surface, leaving plenty of space between the jars. Check all the lids when cool, tightening as needed. If any of the jars did not seal, refrigerate or freeze instead.

Pineapple Salsa

You'll be glad you stocked up on this Pineapple Salsa instead of a generic store-bought version. Scoop it up with your favorite tortilla chips, or pour it over chicken and roast it for a delightful taste sensation.

Sustainable Storage: Lasts up to 1 year.

Makes: about 4 pints

Ingredients

4 (20-ounce) cans crushed pineapple with juice

1 ¼ cups chopped yellow onions

4 medium jalapeño peppers, seeded and finely chopped

1 (28-ounce) can diced tomatoes with juice

¾ cup finely chopped and loosely packed fresh cilantro

Juice and zest of 2 medium limes

½ cup white vinegar

4 tablespoons white balsamic vinegar

3 tablespoons honey

3 medium cloves garlic, peeled and finely minced

1 ½ teaspoons ground cumin

½ teaspoon ground cayenne pepper

1 teaspoon ground coriander

½ teaspoon coarsely ground black pepper

1. In a large stockpot over high heat, combine all ingredients and bring to a boil. Reduce heat to medium-low, and let simmer for 5 minutes. Stir constantly to avoid sticking.

2. Ladle hot salsa into sterilized jars, leaving ¼" headspace at the top of each jar. Make sure to remove all air bubbles. Wipe rims and place sterilized lid on each jar. Tightly screw on sterilized screw bands, and process in a water-bath canner for 15 minutes.

3. Move the jars to a cooling surface, leaving plenty of space between the jars. Check all the lids when cool, tightening as needed. If any of the jars did not seal, refrigerate or freeze instead.

Apple Butter

Preserving fruit butters gives you many wonderful choices for bread and toast, and they can be used in other ways too. In this case, try slathering the butter on a ham or pork chop.

Sustainable Storage:
Lasts up to 1 year.

Makes: 10 pints

Ingredients

8 pounds apples, ends trimmed (do not remove peel or cores)

4 cups apple cider

4 cups firmly packed light brown sugar

4 cups granulated sugar

4 tablespoons ground cinnamon

1 tablespoon ground cloves

1 tablespoon ground nutmeg

1 teaspoon ground cardamom

$\frac{1}{2}$ cup fresh lemon juice

1. Add apples and apple cider to a large stockpot. Cover and simmer until apples are soft. Using a slotted spoon, remove apples; pour cooking liquid into a separate large bowl. Press apples through a sieve or a food mill.

2. Return apple pulp to the stockpot over medium-low heat and add remaining ingredients. Add half the reserved cooking liquid. Cook for 45–60 minutes.

3. As mixture thickens, stir frequently to prevent sticking. If mixture gets too thick, add more reserved cooking liquid until you get the desired consistency.

4. Ladle hot mixture into sterilized jars, leaving $\frac{1}{4}$" headspace at the top of each jar. Make sure to remove all air bubbles. Wipe rims and place sterilized lid on each jar. Tightly screw on sterilized screw bands, and process in a water-bath canner for 10 minutes.

5. Move the jars to a cooling surface, leaving plenty of space between the jars. Check all the lids when cool, tightening as needed. If any of the jars did not seal, refrigerate or freeze instead.

Blueberry Vinegar

Stock this Blueberry Vinegar to add a unique sweet-sour quality to your cooking. Store in bulk and experiment with it!

Sustainable Storage:
Lasts up to 1 year.

Makes: 2 quarts

Ingredients

3 cups fresh blueberries, divided

3 cups rice vinegar

2 (2") cinnamon sticks

4 whole allspice berries

2 tablespoons honey

1. In a large stainless-steel or enamel sauce-pan over high heat, combine $1\frac{1}{2}$ cups blueberries with rice vinegar, cinnamon sticks, and allspice berries. Bring to a boil; reduce heat. Simmer uncovered for 3 minutes. Stir in honey. Remove from heat.

2. Pour mixture through a fine-mesh strainer and let it drain into a large bowl. Discard blueberries, but save allspice berries and cinnamon sticks.

3. Divide remaining $1\frac{1}{2}$ cups blueberries evenly between two sterilized jars. Add 1 cinnamon stick and 2 allspice berries to each jar.

4. Ladle vinegar mixture into two sterilized jars, leaving $\frac{1}{4}$" headspace at the top of each jar. Make sure to remove all air bubbles. Wipe rims and place sterilized lid on each jar. Tightly screw on sterilized screw bands, and process in a water-bath canner for 10 minutes.

5. Move the jars to a cooling surface, leaving plenty of space between the jars. Check all the lids when cool, tightening as needed. If any of the jars did not seal, refrigerate or freeze instead.

6. Let sit in a cool place for 2–3 weeks before opening. Before using, strain through a colander lined with a double layer of cheesecloth; discard solids.

Kiwi Pineapple Preserve

This makes a large quantity that you may want to preserve in small batches, because it won't last long once people get a taste!

Sustainable Storage:
Lasts up to 1 year.

Makes: 15–20 quarts

Ingredients

60 medium kiwis

4 (8-ounce) cans pineapple chunks, drained but with juice reserved

1 (8-ounce) can crushed pineapple, drained but with juice reserved

10 cups granulated sugar

4 tablespoons freshly ground black pepper

1 cup fresh lemon or lime juice

1 cup CLEARJEL

1. Cut kiwis in half and scoop out pulp with a teaspoon. Place pulp in a large stockpot. Add pineapple chunks, crushed pineapple, sugar, pepper, and lemon or lime juice. Stir well.

2. Cover and bring to a boil over high heat. Reduce heat to low and simmer about 30–45 minutes, until kiwi and pineapple are tender but not mushy.

3. Mix CLEARJEL with 1 cup reserved pineapple juice. Add to stockpot and stir well. Simmer another 8 minutes or until mixture thickens.

4. If freezing, cool and transfer into freezer-safe containers, leaving ½" headspace for expansion. If canning, ladle into sterilized jars, leaving ½" headspace at the top of each jar. Make sure to remove all air bubbles. Wipe rims and place sterilized lid on each jar. Tightly screw on sterilized screw bands, and process in a water-bath canner for 20 minutes.

5. Move the jars to a cooling surface, leaving plenty of space between the jars. Check all the lids when cool, tightening as needed. If any of the jars did not seal, refrigerate or freeze instead.

Mouthwatering Mangoes

Can these Mouthwatering Mangoes when they're at their peak ripeness so you can have a taste of summer long after mango season is over.

Sustainable Storage: Lasts up to 1 year.

Makes: 4 pints

Ingredients

6 cups peeled and sliced ripe mangoes

½ tablespoon ground cloves

½ tablespoon ground allspice

½ tablespoon ground ginger

1½ cups white wine or champagne vinegar

1½ cups water

6 cups granulated sugar

4 whole black peppercorns, divided

1. In a large pot over high heat, combine mangoes, cloves, allspice, ginger, vinegar, water, and sugar. Bring to a boil. Reduce heat to low and simmer for about 10 minutes or until the mangoes look semitransparent.

2. In each sterilized jar, put 1 peppercorn, then ladle in mangoes with hot syrup, leaving ½" headspace at the top of each jar. Make sure to remove all air bubbles. Wipe rims and place sterilized lid on each jar. Tightly screw on sterilized screw bands, and process in a water-bath canner for 20 minutes.

3. Move the jars to a cooling surface, leaving plenty of space between the jars. Check all the lids when cool, tightening as needed. If any of the jars did not seal, refrigerate or freeze instead.

Preservation Pointers

If you eat mangoes often, it might be worth it to invest in a mango splitter to help you get rid of the pesky pits. This specialized kitchen tool works just like an apple corer and removes the pit in one easy motion, saving you the trouble of hacking the fruit apart with a knife.

Summer Strawberry Ice Cream

Opt for your own Summer Strawberry Ice Cream for you and your family as you make your own sustainable preserving traditions! If you want to personalize this recipe, try experimenting with a variety of ingredients, like flaked coconut or different berries.

Sustainable Storage:
Lasts up to 1 week.

Makes: 4 cups

Ingredients

$1\frac{1}{4}$ quarts fresh strawberries, hulled

$1\frac{1}{2}$ cups heavy cream, divided

$\frac{3}{4}$ cup granulated sugar

3 large egg yolks

$\frac{1}{2}$ teaspoon vanilla extract

3 tablespoons light corn syrup

1. Place the berries into a blender or food processor; purée until smooth.

2. In a large saucepan over medium heat, heat $1\frac{1}{4}$ cups cream until it begins to bubble at the edges of the pan.

3. While the cream is heating, in a separate bowl, whisk together sugar, egg yolks, remaining $\frac{1}{4}$ cup cream, vanilla, and corn syrup.

4. Slowly pour the heated cream into the egg yolk mixture, whisking constantly.

5. Return the mixture to the saucepan over low heat. Simmer until mixture is thick enough to coat the back of a wooden spoon, about 5 minutes. Do not boil!

6. Remove from heat and stir in the strawberry purée; refrigerate until chilled.

7. Use an ice cream maker and follow the manufacturer's directions to get a really smooth dessert. If you don't have an ice cream maker, you can transfer the custard into a mixing bowl and put it in the freezer. After 30 minutes, beat thoroughly and return to freezer. Repeat until you achieve the desired texture.

Minty Nectarine Pear Preserves

Stock up on these Minty Nectarine Pear Preserves for summer pasta salads, pouring over pork while it roasts, or as a side dish with poultry.

Sustainable Storage: Lasts up to 6 months.

Makes: 5–6 pints

Ingredients

2 pounds pears, peeled and cored

³/₄ cup cold water

¹/₄ cup fresh lemon juice

1 teaspoon whole cloves

1 teaspoon whole allspice berries

2 medium cinnamon sticks

2 pounds ripe nectarines, peeled, pitted, and cut into chunks

5 cups granulated sugar

¹/₂ cup chopped fresh mint, or 2 tablespoons dried mint

1. In a large stockpot, combine pears with water and lemon juice.

2. To make a spice ball, fold a square of cheesecloth twice and place cloves, allspice berries, and cinnamon sticks on the surface. Gather up the corners and tie with kitchen string. Add to stockpot and cook over medium heat for 10 minutes.

3. Add nectarines to a large bowl. Crush fruit with a potato masher. Add sugar and mint; stir well. Add to stockpot.

4. Bring mixture to a boil. Reduce heat to low and simmer for 15 minutes, until mixture is thick. Remove and discard spice ball.

5. If freezing, cool and transfer into freezer-safe containers, leaving ¹/₂" headspace for expansion. If canning, ladle hot preserves into sterilized jars, leaving ¹/₂" headspace at the top of each jar. Make sure to remove all air bubbles. Wipe rims and place sterilized lid on each jar. Tightly screw on sterilized screw bands, and process in a water-bath canner for 15 minutes.

6. Move the jars to a cooling surface, leaving plenty of space between the jars. Check all the lids when cool, tightening as needed. If any of the jars did not seal, refrigerate or freeze instead.

Cranberry Raspberry Sauce

Preserve and keep in your pantry for a seasonal favorite that's yummy all year.

Sustainable Storage:
Lasts up to 1 year.

Makes: 5–6 cups

Ingredients

1 1/4 cups granulated sugar

1/2 cup raspberry vinegar

1/4 cup water

1 (12-ounce) bag fresh cranberries

1 cup fresh raspberries

1 medium cinnamon stick

1 (1/4") vanilla bean

1 tablespoon thinly sliced orange peel

1. In a large nonreactive pan over medium heat, combine sugar, raspberry vinegar, and water. Bring to a boil, stirring constantly until sugar dissolves.

2. Add cranberries, raspberries, cinnamon stick, vanilla bean, and orange peel. Reduce heat to low; cover partially and simmer for 10 minutes, or until cranberries burst.

3. Remove from heat. Remove cinnamon stick and cool completely. Transfer into freezer-safe containers, leaving 1/2" headspace for expansion.

Wine-Poached Figs

When preserving these, be sure to get firm, ripe figs.

Sustainable Storage:
Lasts up to 6 months.

Makes: 6 cups

Ingredients

1 (750-mililiter) bottle pinot noir or Burgundy wine

1 cup dark honey

1/2 cup red wine vinegar or fig vinegar

2 medium cinnamon sticks

2 (1/4") pieces fresh ginger

1 tablespoon whole cloves

2 1/2 pounds fresh ripe figs, quartered

1/8 teaspoon salt

1. In a large nonreactive saucepan over medium heat, combine wine, honey, vinegar, cinnamon sticks, ginger, and cloves. Bring to a simmer and cook until mixture is reduced to a light syrup, about 30–40 minutes. Remove from heat; strain. Discard solids. Return reduction to saucepan over low heat. Add figs and salt.

2. Cook until figs are just tender, 5–10 minutes. Remove from heat; cool before transferring to freezer-safe containers, leaving 1/4" headspace for expansion.

Fundamental Fruit Leather

This basic process will work for nearly any fruit that you'd like to preserve and store as roll-up leather. They have a great shelf life and make wonderful healthy snacks.

Sustainable Storage:
Lasts up to 1 year.

Makes: yield varies

Ingredients

Apples, pears, berries, peaches, or a mixture of your favorite fruit

Honey or granulated sugar

1. Line a dehydrator tray with parchment paper or nonstick silicone sheets.

2. Wash and peel fruit; make sure to remove any overripe parts. Purée fruit in food processor or blender.

3. Taste; sweeten to taste and process again to combine thoroughly.

4. Transfer entire mixture to a saucepan over medium heat. Bring to a low rolling boil; remove from heat and cool.

5. Coat tray for your dehydrator with spray-on oil.

6. Spread an even coating of the purée no more than $1/8$" thick on the prepared dehydrator tray. Dry at 135°F about 12 hours.

7. Wrap in plastic for storing.

8. This process can work in a conventional oven on the lowest setting, but the dehydrator circulates the air so the leathers dry evenly.

Watermelon Pickles

This sustainable southern favorite has a fresh, thirst-quenching quality.

Sustainable Storage:
Lasts up to 1 year.

Makes: 5 pints

Ingredients

4 pounds watermelon rinds, pink parts trimmed, cubed

½ cup canning and pickling salt

8 cups water

4 cups granulated sugar

2 cups white vinegar

5 (½") cinnamon sticks

10 whole cloves

5 (¼") slices peeled fresh ginger

1 medium lemon, cut into 5 slices

1. In a large stockpot, combine watermelon rinds, pickling salt, and enough water to cover. Put a plate on top of watermelon so it stays submerged in brine; let sit overnight. Drain and rinse thoroughly.

2. In a large pot over medium-low heat, place rind along with enough water to cover. Simmer until tender, being careful not to overcook.

3. In a separate large stockpot over medium-low heat, combine remaining ingredients, including 8 cups water. Simmer for 10 minutes.

4. Add watermelon rind to stockpot, cooking over low heat until nearly transparent.

5. Pack rind and hot liquid into half-pint sterilized jars, leaving ½" headspace at the top of each jar. Make sure to remove all air bubbles. Wipe rims and place sterilized lid on each jar. Tightly screw on sterilized screw bands, and process in a water-bath canner for 10 minutes.

6. Move the jars to a cooling surface, leaving plenty of space between the jars. Check all the lids when cool, tightening as needed. If any of the jars did not seal, refrigerate or freeze instead.

Pickled Peaches and Pears

If you're making in bulk, save some time and prepare your sterilized quart jars beforehand: Put 1 whole stick of cinnamon, 2 whole cloves, and 1 slice of ginger in each jar.

Sustainable Storage:
Lasts up to 1 year.

Makes: 4 quarts

Ingredients

5 cups granulated sugar

2½ cups white vinegar

2½ cups water

4 medium cinnamon sticks

8 whole cloves

4 (¼") slices peeled fresh ginger

8 cups chopped peeled peaches

8 cups chopped peeled pears

1. In a large stockpot over medium heat, combine sugar, vinegar, water, cinnamon sticks, cloves, and ginger. Bring to a boil. Reduce heat to low and simmer for 10 minutes, then add peaches and pears. Continue cooking until partially tender.

2. Pack fruit into sterilized jars, leaving ½" headspace at the top of each jar. Pour in hot syrup, reserving headspace. Make sure to remove all air bubbles. Wipe rims and place sterilized lid on each jar. Tightly screw on sterilized screw bands, and process in a water-bath canner for 10 minutes.

3. Move the jars to a cooling surface, leaving plenty of space between the jars. Check all the lids when cool, tightening as needed. If any of the jars did not seal, refrigerate or freeze instead.

Candied Fruit Rinds

Preserving for self-sustainability doesn't mean giving up sweets! Preserve and enjoy these Candied Fruit Rinds as treats for you and your family.

Sustainable Storage:
Lasts up to 1 year.

Makes: 20 slices

Ingredients

1 large navel orange

1 medium grapefruit

2 medium lemons or 2 large limes

¼ cup water

⅛ teaspoon salt

¼ cup honey

¾ cup granulated sugar

1 tablespoon superfine sugar

1. Set a baking rack over a sheet of waxed paper. Set aside.

2. Carefully remove peels from fruits; remove as much pith as possible. In a medium saucepan over medium-high heat, combine peels with enough water to cover. Bring to a full boil; reduce heat to low and simmer for 30 minutes. Drain peels. Refill saucepan with fresh water and repeat cooking process; this reduces bitterness.

3. Drain and cool citrus peels. Slice into strips about ¼" thick.

4. In a medium saucepan over low heat, combine ¼ cup water, salt, honey, and granulated sugar; bring to a simmer. Add peels to saucepan; continue simmering about 25 minutes.

5. Turn off heat; let rinds sit in syrup until syrup cools. Remove rind pieces from syrup; dry on prepared baking rack. Sprinkle with superfine sugar and store in an airtight container.

Candied Pineapple Chunks

Preserve and stock these Candied Pineapple Chunks for a luscious snack, or you can use them in making fruitcake!

Sustainable Storage:
Lasts up to 1 year.

Makes: yield varies

Ingredients

2 cups granulated sugar

1 cup water

1 teaspoon ground ginger

$\frac{1}{3}$ cup light corn syrup

1 medium ripe pineapple, peeled, cored, and chopped into bite-sized pieces

1. Set a baking rack over a sheet of waxed paper. Set aside.

2. In a large saucepan over medium-high heat, combine sugar, water, ginger, and corn syrup. Bring to a boil; reduce heat to low. Add pineapple and simmer until pineapple turns translucent.

3. Drain pineapple and allow to dry on prepared baking rack. Store in an airtight container.

CHAPTER ELEVEN

Meat, Poultry, and Fish

Chili with Meat

Can and preserve this Chili with Meat, and when you're ready to serve it as a meal, add cooked pinto or kidney beans and heat through.

Sustainable Storage:
Lasts up to 1 year.

Makes: 6 quarts

Ingredients

10 pounds lean ground beef

3 medium cloves garlic, peeled and minced

4 cups chopped onions

4 tablespoons extra-virgin olive oil

4 (35-ounce) cans chopped tomatoes

½ cup chili powder

1 teaspoon cumin seeds

2 medium jalapeño peppers, seeded and minced

2 teaspoons dried oregano

4 teaspoons honey

2 teaspoons onion powder

1 teaspoon freshly ground black pepper

1. In a large stockpot over medium heat, sauté ground beef, garlic, and chopped onions in olive oil until meat is browned. Drain excess fat; return to stockpot.

2. Add remaining ingredients; simmer for 20 minutes.

3. Ladle hot chili into sterilized jars, leaving 1" headspace at the top of each jar. Make sure to remove all air bubbles. Wipe rims and place sterilized lid on each jar. Tightly screw on sterilized screw bands, and process at 11 pounds of pressure in a pressure canner for 75 minutes for pints and 90 minutes for quarts.

4. Move the jars to a cooling surface, leaving plenty of space between the jars. Check all the lids when cool, tightening as needed. If any of the jars did not seal, refrigerate or freeze instead.

Ready-to-Go Ribs

The process is a little lengthy, but it's well worth the effort. When you take these out of the freezer, they only need a quick broil or toss on the grill.

Sustainable Storage:
Lasts up to 6 months.

Makes: 3 pounds

Rub Ingredients

3 pounds pork spareribs
$\frac{1}{2}$ cup firmly packed dark brown sugar
$\frac{1}{4}$ cup paprika
1 tablespoon freshly ground black pepper
1 tablespoon salt
1 tablespoon chili powder
1 tablespoon garlic powder
1 tablespoon onion powder
1 tablespoon freshly grated lemon zest
1 tablespoon freshly grated orange zest
1 tablespoon dried basil
1 teaspoon mesquite powder
1 teaspoon ground cayenne pepper

Sauce Ingredients

1 cup ketchup
$\frac{1}{4}$ cup whiskey
$\frac{1}{4}$ cup molasses
$\frac{1}{4}$ cup vinegar
2 tablespoons extra-virgin olive oil
1 tablespoon chili powder
1 tablespoon ground ginger
1 tablespoon Worcestershire sauce
1 tablespoon prepared hearty mustard
2 medium cloves garlic, peeled and minced
$\frac{1}{2}$ teaspoon crushed red pepper flakes

1. Preheat oven to 200°F. Line a 9" x 13" baking sheet with foil or parchment paper.

2. Remove membrane from underside of ribs. Trim off any loose fat. In a small bowl, combine all rub ingredients. Rub both sides of ribs with mixture.

3. Wrap ribs in plastic wrap, followed by aluminum foil; roast in oven for 4 hours. Cool.

4. While ribs cook, prepare sauce. In a medium saucepan over low heat, combine all sauce ingredients. Simmer about 1 hour. The sauce will reduce a bit during this time.

5. Preheat grill. Remove wrap from ribs and cook until internal temperature reaches 145°F. Brush with sauce on each turn.

6. Allow to cool. Cut into single-serving sizes, wrapping with freezer-safe plastic wrap and covering again with aluminum foil.

Mama's Meatloaf

This may be frozen whole, but preserving in portions allows family members to defrost and eat one piece at a time as desired. If you like, add a portion of mashed potatoes on top of the spaghetti sauce for a heartier meal.

Sustainable Storage:
Lasts 3–4 months.

Makes: 8 servings

Ingredients

1 1/2 pounds lean ground beef

1/2 cup bread crumbs

1 medium onion, peeled and minced

1/4 cup minced green bell pepper

2 tablespoons molasses

1 tablespoon prepared steak sauce

1 large egg, slightly beaten

2 medium stalks celery, trimmed and finely chopped

1 tablespoon Worcestershire sauce

2 medium cloves garlic, peeled and chopped

1 1/2 teaspoons salt

1/8 teaspoon freshly ground black pepper

1/4 cup prepared spaghetti sauce

1. Preheat the oven to 350°F. Spray an 8" × 8" baking pan with nonstick cooking spray.

2. In a large bowl, thoroughly combine all ingredients except spaghetti sauce.

3. Press meat mixture into prepared pan. Top with spaghetti sauce.

4. Bake for 1 hour, or until slightly brown around the edges.

5. Slice meatloaf into eight pieces; freeze whole, or freeze individual pieces double-wrapped in freezer-safe wrapping.

Barbecued Pork

Make the most of this old-fashioned Barbecued Pork. Preserve some for sandwiches and the rest for a barbecue-flavored stew. You can substitute an equal amount of chicken for the pork if you desire.

Sustainable Storage: Lasts up to 6 months.

Makes: about 7 quarts

Ingredients

2 cups barbecue sauce

2 cups ketchup

2 tablespoons white vinegar

2 tablespoons granulated sugar

$\frac{1}{8}$ teaspoon salt

$\frac{1}{8}$ teaspoon freshly ground black pepper

1 tablespoon finely minced garlic

2 beef bouillon cubes, crumbled

1 bunch green onions, trimmed and finely chopped

6–8 pounds boneless pork roast

1. Spray a 9" × 13" baking pan with nonstick cooking spray. Set aside.

2. In a large bowl, combine all ingredients except green onions and pork. Whisk together until well combined; stir in green onions.

3. Cut pork into bite-sized pieces. Place in prepared baking pan; pour marinade over top.

4. Cover with heavy-duty aluminum foil; refrigerate overnight.

5. The next day, preheat the oven to 350°F. Roast pork for 30–40 minutes, until pork is fully cooked. Cool.

6. Transfer into freezer-safe containers, leaving $\frac{1}{2}$" headspace for expansion. Add more barbecue sauce if you need it to cover the meat in the containers.

Mango Steaks

For an alternative preserving method, simply marinate the flank steak in the sauce and freeze it before cooking. This allows the steak to marinate while you defrost it. In this case, using a vacuum sealer works great.

Sustainable Storage:
Lasts up to 6 months.

Makes: 4–6 servings

Ingredients

1 medium peach, peeled, pitted, and chopped

$\frac{1}{4}$ cup extra-virgin olive oil

2 cups mango juice

1 tablespoon garlic salt

2 tablespoons Worcestershire sauce

2 teaspoons kosher salt

1 tablespoon freshly ground black pepper

$\frac{1}{4}$ cup red wine

$\frac{1}{4}$ cup soy sauce

$\frac{1}{4}$ cup honey

3–4 pounds flank steak

1. In a food processor or blender, process chopped peach until puréed.

2. In a medium saucepan over low heat, combine peach purée with all remaining ingredients except for steak. Heat until warm.

3. Pour half the sauce into the bottom of a marinating dish, place the steak on top, and pour the remainder over the top. Cover and marinate in the refrigerator for 24 hours.

4. Spray the grill with olive oil and preheat. Remove steaks from marinade and grill until they reach 120°F internally (rare), brushing with sauce frequently.

5. Cool and wrap in plastic, then place each steak in a freezer-safe bag. When ready to use, defrost and heat. If you like your steak rare, just do a quick warm-up in a skillet. Otherwise you can defrost and cook each steak to your liking.

Pasta Sauce

As is true of taco sauce, making your own preserved Pasta Sauce comes in very handy for many dishes.

Sustainable Storage:
Lasts 4–6 months.

Makes: 8 quarts

Ingredients

40 pounds tomatoes, cored and chopped into small pieces

2½ cups finely chopped fresh basil, divided

½ cup finely chopped fresh thyme, divided

½ cup finely chopped fresh rosemary, divided

1 cup finely chopped fresh oregano, divided

2 pounds lean ground beef

2 medium green bell peppers, seeded and diced

3 tablespoons freshly ground black pepper

2 cups chopped onions

3 tablespoons extra-virgin olive oil

1 cup fresh lemon juice, divided

1½ cups granulated sugar, divided

⅛ teaspoon salt, divided

1. Put tomatoes in a food processor or blender and purée in small batches. Divide puréed tomatoes between two large stockpots.

2. Divide herbs equally between stockpots.

3. In a large skillet over medium heat, working in batches if necessary, sauté ground beef, bell peppers, black pepper, and onions in olive oil until meat is browned and vegetables are soft. Drain well in a colander to remove excess fat. Split mixture evenly between the stockpots.

4. Set stockpots over high heat and bring to a boil. Divide lemon juice, sugar, and salt evenly between the pots. Reduce heat to low and simmer for 45–60 minutes, stirring often.

5. Cool and transfer into freezer-safe containers, leaving ¼" headspace for expansion.

Sloppy Joes

Kids and adults alike will love this sloppy, tasty mix. Preserve in bulk and serve with rolls à la sloppy joes or as filling for a unique lasagna!

Sustainable Storage:
Lasts 6–8 months.

Makes: 8 quarts

Ingredients

5 pounds lean ground beef

2 large green bell peppers, seeded and finely chopped

2 large onions, peeled and finely chopped

3–4 tablespoons extra-virgin olive oil

1 $\frac{1}{3}$ cups ketchup

1 cup water

4 tablespoons fresh lemon juice

2 tablespoons firmly packed dark brown sugar

2 beef bouillon cubes, crumbled

2 teaspoons salt

2 teaspoons freshly ground black pepper

1 teaspoon mustard powder

2 teaspoons granulated sugar

2 teaspoons white vinegar

1 teaspoon chili powder or Tabasco sauce

1. In a large skillet, working in batches if necessary, sauté ground beef, green pepper, and onions in olive oil until meat is browned and onions and peppers are soft. Drain well in a colander to remove excess fat.

2. In a large stockpot over low heat, combine drained meat mixture with remaining ingredients. Simmer for 20 minutes.

3. Cool and transfer into freezer-safe containers, leaving $\frac{1}{4}$" headspace for expansion.

Homemade Salami

You'll love this Homemade Salami compared to the overprocessed store-bought versions. For the recipe to succeed, you must use curing salt or Tender Quick.

Sustainable Storage:
Lasts up to 1 week in refrigerator.

Makes: 6–8 small rolls

Ingredients

5 pounds ground beef

5 teaspoons salt

5 hot peppercorns, crushed

2 teaspoons garlic powder

1 1/2 teaspoons whole yellow mustard seeds

2 1/2 teaspoons hickory-smoked salt

2 teaspoons onion powder

5 teaspoons curing salt or Morton Tender Quick home meat cure

2 teaspoons ground caraway seeds

1. In a very large bowl or pot, combine all ingredients. Knead for 5 minutes. Cover tightly with plastic wrap; refrigerate 24 hours.

2. Knead mixture again for 5 minutes. Cover tightly with plastic wrap; refrigerate another 24 hours.

3. Preheat the oven to 150°F. Knead mixture once more for 5 minutes; form into 6–8 small rolls. Place on a broiler pan and bake for 8 hours, turning every hour. Turn oven off; let salami cool on broiler rack while remaining in the oven until it reaches room temperature.

4. Wrap tightly in plastic wrap. Refrigerate and slice. Serve on crackers or bread.

Sauerbraten

Preserve this Sauerbraten for a sustainable and tasty meal for you and your family. This pickled beef is traditionally served with potatoes, dumplings, or cabbage. It can be frozen or canned using pressure-canning methods for beef.

Sustainable Storage:
Lasts up to 3 months in the freezer or up to 1 year when canned.

Makes: 4 pounds

Marinade Ingredients

1 cup red wine

1 cup red wine vinegar

2 cups water

1 medium onion, peeled and sliced

1 tablespoon crushed peppercorns

1 tablespoon crushed juniper berries

2 dried bay leaves

1 teaspoon whole yellow mustard seeds

1 teaspoon canning and pickling salt

1 teaspoon grated fresh ginger

Roast and Braising Sauce Ingredients

3 pounds shank or pot roast

1 1/2 tablespoons salted butter

1 1/2 tablespoons extra-virgin olive oil

2 cups diced red onions

1 1/2 cups diced celery

2 cups diced carrots

1/2 cup all-purpose flour

Sauerbraten cont.

1. In a large saucepan over high heat, combine all marinade ingredients. Bring to a boil and boil for 10 minutes. Cool.

2. Place beef in a large container or dish and pour marinade over top to cover. If necessary, add more wine to cover beef. Marinate in refrigerator for 3 days, turning meat regularly.

3. Drain meat, reserving marinade. Strain marinade and set aside.

4. Preheat the oven to 350°F.

5. Set a stovetop-safe roasting pan over medium heat (you may need to put it over two burners). Add butter and heat until melted. Add meat, pour olive oil on top, and brown on all sides. Add reserved marinade. Toss vegetables lightly in flour; add to roasting pan. Cover and transfer pan to the oven. Roast for $1\frac{1}{4}$ hours. You may add water to this if needed at any time to prevent the juices from reducing too much.

6. If freezing, transfer sauerbraten to freezer-safe containers, leaving $\frac{1}{4}$" headspace for expansion. If canning, pack into sterilized jars, leaving 1" headspace at the top of each jar. Make sure to remove all air bubbles. Wipe rims and place sterilized lid on each jar. Tightly screw on sterilized screw bands, and process at 10 pounds of pressure in a pressure canner for 75 minutes for pints and 90 minutes for quarts.

Teriyaki Jerky

Making your own jerky is very cost-efficient, and the shrinkage is minimal. This recipe is fantastic for any type of meat that you enjoy with a rich teriyaki flavor.

Sustainable Storage:
Lasts up to 2 months.

Makes: 3½ pounds

Ingredients

5 pounds meat

2½ cups soy sauce

2½ cups teriyaki sauce

3 tablespoons firmly packed dark brown sugar

3 tablespoons garlic powder

3 tablespoons onion powder

2 tablespoons ground ginger

1 (5-ounce) bottle liquid smoke

½ cup honey

5 teaspoons curing salt

1. Slice meat as thinly as possible (a mandoline or meat slicer helps with this). About $^3/_{16}$" is recommended. Put meat slices into a large marinating dish.

2. In a large bowl, combine remaining ingredients until well blended. Pour over meat.

3. Cover and refrigerate for 24–48 hours, stirring regularly. Drain meat completely.

4. If using a dehydrator, put an equal number of slices on each tray, being careful not to let slices touch. Follow manufacturer's recommended temperatures and times.

5. If drying in the oven, lay the meat on a rack over a baking tray and set your oven to 150°F. Turn regularly over the next 6 hours.

6. Cool and store in an airtight container or food-storage bag.

Barbecued Turkey Drumsticks

Be self-sufficient with what you have! If you find you don't have enough sauce for canning, add equal amounts ketchup and water.

Sustainable Storage:
Lasts up to 1 year.

Makes: 7–8 quarts

Ingredients

2 cups of your favorite commercial barbecue sauce

2 cups ketchup

2 tablespoons white vinegar

2 tablespoons granulated sugar

$\frac{1}{8}$ teaspoon salt

$\frac{1}{8}$ teaspoon freshly ground black pepper

1 tablespoon finely minced garlic

2 beef bouillon cubes, crumbled

1 medium bunch green onions, trimmed and finely chopped

6–8 large turkey drumsticks, skinned

1. Spray a large baking pan with nonstick cooking spray. Set aside.

2. In a large bowl, combine all ingredients except turkey legs and green onions. Whisk together until well combined. Stir in green onions.

3. Put drumsticks in prepared baking pan. Pour marinade over drumsticks. Cover with heavy-duty aluminum foil; refrigerate overnight.

4. Preheat oven to 350°F. Roast drumsticks in oven 1–1½ hours, or until they are cooked through. Remove drumsticks from sauce; reserve sauce. Allow drumsticks to cool.

5. Debone drumsticks and chop meat into bite-sized pieces. Stir meat back into sauce and bring to a simmer. Remove from heat and ladle into sterilized jars, leaving 1" headspace at the top of each jar. Make sure to remove all air bubbles. Wipe rims and place sterilized lid on each jar. Tightly screw on sterilized screw bands, and process at 10 pounds of pressure in a pressure canner for 75 minutes for pints and 90 minutes for quarts.

6. Move the jars to a cooling surface, leaving plenty of space between the jars. Check all the lids when cool, tightening as needed. If any of the jars did not seal, refrigerate or freeze instead.

Cider Ham

To serve, simply defrost and warm at 350°F for about 20 minutes.

Sustainable Storage:
Lasts 6–8 months.

Makes: 6 servings

Ingredients

4 cups apple cider

½ cup firmly packed light brown sugar

1 teaspoon dry mustard powder or stone-ground mustard

1 teaspoon freshly grated orange zest

1 (4-pound) cooked whole ham

6 ring-shaped slices pineapple, divided

6 tablespoons salted butter, divided

1. In a large bowl, combine cider, brown sugar, mustard, and orange zest.

2. Cut the ham into 6 steaks, trimming excess fat. Place steaks in large marinating dish and pour cider mixture over the top. Cover and marinate overnight in the refrigerator, turning occasionally.

3. Individually wrap each steak topped with a slice of pineapple and a tablespoon of butter. Brush the top with marinade. Place steaks in a freezer-safe container.

Pickled Chicken

This is a quick-pickling method intended for immediate use.

Sustainable Storage:
Lasts 1 week in the refrigerator or up to 1 year if canned with brine.

Makes: 4 pounds

Ingredients

1 whole (4-pound) roasting chicken, cut into pieces

2 cups white vinegar

2 cups balsamic vinegar

1 medium onion, peeled and sliced

1 tablespoon canning and pickling salt

1 dried bay leaf

6 whole cloves

12 whole black peppercorns

1 medium bunch fresh dill

1. In a large stockpot over high heat, place chicken pieces and add enough water to cover. Add white vinegar and balsamic vinegar; bring to a boil. Skim excess fat off the top of the water.

2. Lower to medium heat and add onion, canning salt, bay leaf, cloves, peppercorns, and dill. Cook until chicken is tender.

Refrigerator-Pickled Herring

Preserve for self-sustainability and for tradition! This is a common side dish and snack in Scandinavia during Christmas and midsummer celebrations.

Sustainable Storage:
Lasts up to 3 weeks in the refrigerator.

Makes: 2 pounds

Ingredients

2 pounds salt herring fillets

$\frac{3}{4}$ cup water, plus more for soaking fillets

$\frac{1}{2}$ cup white vinegar

$\frac{1}{3}$ cup apple cider vinegar

1 dried bay leaf

$\frac{1}{4}$ teaspoon whole black peppercorns

$\frac{1}{4}$ teaspoon whole allspice berries

$\frac{1}{4}$ teaspoon dill seeds

$\frac{1}{2}$ medium cinnamon stick

$\frac{1}{3}$ cup granulated sugar

1 medium red onion, peeled and sliced

1. Soak fillets in water in refrigerator for 6 hours; change water and soak for 6 hours more. Rinse and slice into bite-sized pieces.

2. In a medium saucepan over high heat, combine remaining ingredients except onion. Bring to a boil, stirring regularly. Remove from heat.

3. Layer onion slices into sterilized jars with fish. Add pickling mixture and cap. Let age about 1 week in the refrigerator before serving.

CHAPTER TWELVE

Nuts, Spices, and Herbs

Nutty Honey Peanut Butter

Try a little vanilla extract in this recipe for a nice twist. Preserve and store several batches with different nuts of your choice!

Sustainable Storage:
Lasts up to 6 months.

Makes: about 3 cups

Ingredients

2 cups roasted peanuts

2 tablespoons vegetable oil

1 cup honey

$\frac{1}{8}$ teaspoon salt

1. Put nuts through a blender or chopper. Transfer 1 cup chopped nuts to a small bowl.

2. Add vegetable oil to nuts in small bowl; mix thoroughly. Add more oil if mixture is not smooth enough.

3. Add honey and salt; mix thoroughly. Add remaining nuts and mix until evenly distributed.

4. Pack into sterilized jars, leaving 1" head-space at the top of each jar. Make sure to remove all air bubbles. Wipe rims and place sterilized lid on each jar. Tightly screw on sterilized screw bands, and process in a water-bath canner for 60 minutes.

5. Move the jars to a cooling surface, leaving plenty of space between the jars. Check all the lids when cool, tightening as needed. If any of the jars did not seal, refrigerate or freeze instead.

6. It's natural for oil to separate while jars sit. When you serve, mix the peanut butter.

Just Nutty!

This recipe is for nut lovers who just want to keep a wonderful nutty snack on hand. However, you can season the nuts with butter, Worcestershire sauce, garlic salt, seasoned salt, or another favorite flavoring before canning.

Sustainable Storage:
Lasts up to 1 year.

Makes: 6 cups

Ingredients

1 cup shelled pecans

1 cup shelled peanuts

1 cup shelled walnuts

1 cup shelled almonds

1 cup shelled filberts

1 cup shelled Brazil nuts

1. Preheat the oven to 250°F. Spread nuts evenly in a single layer in a large baking pan.

2. Bake for 15–20 minutes or until nuts are dry. Be careful not to brown or burn them.

3. Pack into sterilized pint jars, leaving $\frac{1}{2}$" headspace at the top of each jar. Place sterilized lid on each jar. Tightly screw on sterilized screw bands and process in a water-bath canner, leaving 1" of the jars above water. Process for 30 minutes.

4. Move the jars to a cooling surface, leaving plenty of space between the jars. Check all the lids when cool, tightening as needed.

Plum and Walnut Preserves

Can these Plum and Walnut Preserves when your plums are in season, and you'll have them to enjoy during the winter months. The rum-plum blend makes them warm, welcoming, and reminiscent of holiday flavors.

Sustainable Storage:
Lasts up to 3 months.

Makes: 9½ pints

Ingredients

4 pounds fresh plums, pitted and quartered

4 medium limes, very thinly sliced

1½ cups golden raisins

7 cups granulated sugar

2 cups chopped walnuts

8 tablespoons dark rum

1. In a large stockpot over low heat, combine plums, limes, raisins, and sugar. Cook gently for about 45 minutes, stirring constantly, until the mixture is thickened.

2. Remove from heat and stir in walnuts and rum. Let stand about 5 minutes.

3. Ladle into sterilized jars, leaving ¼" headspace at the top of each jar. Make sure to remove all air bubbles. Wipe rims and place sterilized lid on each jar. Tightly screw on sterilized screw bands, and process in a water-bath canner for 10 minutes.

4. Move the jars to a cooling surface, leaving plenty of space between the jars. Check all the lids when cool, tightening as needed. If any of the jars did not seal, refrigerate or freeze instead.

Sweet Walnuts

The nice part about this dish is that once you get it started, it pretty much takes care of itself, making a nice snack that can be saved and preserved.

Sustainable Storage: Lasts up to 6 months in the freezer.

Makes: 1 pound

Ingredients

1 pound shelled walnuts

½ cup (8 tablespoons) salted butter

½ cup firmly packed light brown sugar

1½ teaspoons ground cinnamon

¼ teaspoon ground allspice

¼ teaspoon ground ginger

¼ teaspoon vanilla extract

1. Place all ingredients into a slow cooker; stir.

2. Cook on high setting for 15 minutes. Reduce to lowest setting and continue cooking uncovered for 2 hours. Nuts are done when glaze isn't sticky and nuts have a crisp texture.

3. Cool and transfer to freezer-safe containers.

Pickled Walnuts

Preserve these Pickled Walnuts for a wide variety of unique additions to meals, especially for barbecued venison and other game animals.

Sustainable Storage:
Lasts up to 1 year.

Makes: 5 pounds

Ingredients

5 pounds shelled fresh black walnuts

2 cups canning and pickling salt, divided

1 quart malt vinegar

$2\frac{1}{4}$ cups firmly packed light brown sugar

1 teaspoon ground allspice

1 teaspoon ground cloves

1 teaspoon ground cinnamon

1 teaspoon ground ginger

1. Pierce each nut with a fork in several places. Place walnuts in a large bowl along with water to cover and 1 cup canning salt. Place a weight on top so the nuts stay submerged below the brine. Let set 7 days.

2. Drain and make a fresh brine with water and remaining canning salt. Let stand another 7 days.

3. Dry the walnuts on a tray using a light cloth over the top to keep dust and dirt out. When the nuts turn black, they're ready for the pickle solution.

4. In a medium saucepan over high heat, combine vinegar, brown sugar, allspice, cloves, cinnamon, and ginger. Bring to a boil. Add nuts, reduce heat to low, and simmer for 15 minutes.

5. Pack nuts and hot syrup into sterilized jars, leaving $\frac{1}{2}$" headspace at the top of each jar. Make sure to remove all air bubbles. Wipe rims and place sterilized lid on each jar. Tightly screw on sterilized screw bands, and process in a water-bath canner for 10 minutes for pints and 15 minutes for quarts.

6. Move the jars to a cooling surface, leaving plenty of space between the jars. Check all the lids when cool, tightening as needed. If any of the jars did not seal, refrigerate or freeze instead.

Candied Ginger

Having Candied Ginger handy is wonderful for spontaneous baking, and it also makes a handy breath mint! Note that this basic process also works effectively for fruit, particularly pineapple.

Sustainable Storage:
Lasts up to 2 years.

Makes: 4 pints

Ingredients

2 pounds fresh ginger, peeled and cut into very thin strips across the grain

2 cups cold water

1 tablespoon freshly grated lemon zest

4 cups granulated sugar

2 cups superfine sugar

1. In a medium saucepan over high heat, add ginger slices and enough cold water to cover. Bring to a boil, then reduce heat to low. Simmer for 5 minutes. Drain.

2. Repeat procedure with fresh cold water to cover. Drain and set out on paper towels to dry.

3. In a large stockpot over high heat, combine 2 cups cold water, lemon zest, and granulated sugar. Bring to a boil, then reduce heat to low. Simmer for 10 minutes, or until a syrup forms.

4. Add ginger. Cook slowly over low heat until all syrup is absorbed, 40–50 minutes. Do not boil.

5. Remove ginger; place on a wire rack to dry.

6. Spread superfine sugar on waxed paper. Roll ginger in superfine sugar; let ginger stand in the sugar until it crystallizes. Spoon into cold sterilized jars. Cap and seal.

Garlic Onion Pesto

You'll want to have this Garlic Onion Pesto on hand for a great white pizza when you want it. Just brush it over the crust and add your favorite toppings.

Sustainable Storage:
Lasts up to 6 months.

Makes: about 3 cups

Ingredients
2 cups fresh chopped basil
¼ cup pine nuts
¼ cup dried minced onion
2 tablespoons minced garlic
¼ cup extra-virgin olive oil
1 tablespoon fresh lemon juice

1. In a medium nonreactive saucepan over low heat, combine all ingredients. Simmer for 15 minutes.
2. Cool; transfer to ice cube trays. Freeze.
3. When frozen, pop out frozen pesto cubes and put in a food-storage bag in the freezer.

Parsley, Sage, Rosemary, and Thyme

This is a great Italian herb blend to preserve if you grow your own herbs. If you don't, head to a farmers' market for the freshest herbs.

Sustainable Storage:
Lasts up to 1 year.

Makes: 3½ cups

Ingredients
½ cup blanched and minced fresh rosemary
1 cup blanched and minced fresh sage
1 cup blanched and minced fresh thyme
1 cup blanched and minced fresh parsley

Freeze in small plastic containers or add herbs to olive oil and freeze in ice cube trays. When frozen, pop out cubes and put in a food-storage bag in the freezer.

Pickled Garlic and Onions

This sustainable recipe makes a nice snack or may be used in garnishing various beverages.

Sustainable Storage:
Lasts up to 1 year.

Makes: 2½ pints

Ingredients

12 large cloves garlic, blanched for 30 seconds and peeled

12 pearl onions, blanched for 30 seconds and peeled

2 cups white vinegar

½ cup red wine vinegar

1 cup dry white wine

1 tablespoon canning and pickling salt

1 tablespoon granulated sugar

1 tablespoon dried oregano or basil

1. Set aside garlic and onions after blanching.

2. In a medium nonreactive saucepan over high heat, combine all remaining ingredients. Bring to a boil and let boil for 1 minute.

3. Fill sterilized jars evenly with garlic and onions. Pour hot brine over onions and garlic, leaving ½" headspace at the top of each jar. Make sure to remove all air bubbles. Wipe rims and place sterilized lid on each jar. Tightly screw on sterilized screw bands, and process in a water-bath canner for 10 minutes.

4. Move the jars to a cooling surface, leaving plenty of space between the jars. Check all the lids when cool, tightening as needed. If any of the jars did not seal, refrigerate or freeze instead.

Pickled Capers

Bring the fresh Mediterranean taste of capers to your preserved food stock! If you buy salted capers, rinse them before you pickle them or they'll be way too salty.

Sustainable Storage:
Lasts up to 1 year.

Makes: 1 quart

Ingredients

3 cups capers

4 cups white vinegar

2 teaspoons canning and pickling salt

1 medium red or Spanish onion, peeled and thinly sliced

$\frac{1}{2}$ medium lemon, thinly sliced

1 teaspoon pickling spice

2 medium cloves garlic, peeled and minced

5 whole black peppercorns

$\frac{1}{2}$ teaspoon celery seeds

$\frac{1}{2}$ teaspoon whole yellow mustard seeds

1. In a medium saucepan over high heat, combine all ingredients. Bring to a boil and continue to boil for 5 minutes.

2. Pack into a sterilized quart jar, leaving $\frac{1}{4}$" headspace at the top of the jar. Make sure to remove all air bubbles. Wipe rim and place sterilized lid on the jar. Tightly screw on a sterilized screw band, and process in a water-bath canner for 15 minutes.

3. Move the jar to a cooling surface. Check the lid when cool, tightening as needed. If the jar did not seal, refrigerate or freeze instead.

Herb Garlic Blend

Preserve this Herb Garlic Blend and mix with butter for garlic bread beyond compare.

Sustainable Storage:
Lasts up to 1 year.

Makes: 1 cup

Ingredients

4 tablespoons dried basil

4 tablespoons dried tarragon

4 tablespoons dried chervil

5 tablespoons dried thyme

1 teaspoon garlic powder

1. Put all ingredients into a blender or food processor; process until combined.
2. Store in a jar with an airtight cover.

Sloppy Joe Seasoning Mix

Having this Sloppy Joe Seasoning Mix is super helpful for an easy weeknight dinner. If you are canning the mix, eliminate the cornstarch so the sauce isn't too thick to process properly. When making sloppy joes, use 3 tablespoons seasoning mix to 1 pound ground meat.

Sustainable Storage:
Lasts up to 3 years.

Makes: about $1\frac{1}{4}$ cups

Ingredients

1 cup dried minced onion

3 tablespoons dried green bell pepper flakes

4 teaspoons salt

3 tablespoons cornstarch

4 teaspoons garlic powder

2 teaspoons mustard powder

2 teaspoons celery seeds

2 teaspoons chili powder

In a small bowl, combine all ingredients until well blended. Store in an airtight container in a cool, dark area.

Apple Pie Spice

Preserving this Apple Pie Spice means adding warm flavor to many more dishes than just apple pie. Experiment by adding to your favorite seasonal drinks and desserts.

Sustainable Storage:
Lasts up to 3 years.

Makes: about 2 tablespoons

Ingredients

1 tablespoon ground cinnamon

1 1/2 teaspoons ground nutmeg

1 teaspoon ground allspice

1/4 teaspoon ground cloves

Place all ingredients in a jar; cover tightly and shake well to mix. Store in an airtight container in a cool, dark area.

Pumpkin Pie Spice

An American classic that you can preserve and use again and again! You'll notice the difference with this homemade Pumpkin Pie Spice compared to the store-bought version. When making pumpkin pie, use 3 1/4 teaspoons Pumpkin Pie Spice per 1 1/2 cups canned pumpkin.

Sustainable Storage:
Lasts up to 3 years.

Makes: 1 cup

Ingredients

1/2 cup ground cinnamon

1/4 cup ground ginger

2 tablespoons ground nutmeg

2 tablespoons ground cloves

Place all ingredients in a jar; cover tightly and shake well to mix. Store in an airtight container in a cool, dark area.

Chili Seasoning Mix

When making chili, use $\frac{1}{2}$ cup Chili Seasoning Mix for every 1 pound ground beef.

Sustainable Storage:
Lasts up to 3 years.

Makes: $1\frac{1}{4}$ cups

Ingredients

6 tablespoons chili powder

4 tablespoons onion powder

2 tablespoons ground cumin

2 tablespoons garlic powder

2 tablespoons dried oregano (preferably Mexican)

2 tablespoons cornstarch

2 tablespoons paprika

1 teaspoon celery seeds

Add all ingredients to a 1-pint Mason jar. Put on lid and screw band, and shake until well combined. Store in jar with a tight-fitting lid in a cool, dark area.

Spaghetti Herb Mix

Make this Spaghetti Herb Mix in bulk to use for easy weeknight meals. Use $\frac{1}{2}$ cup dry mix for every 1 pound ground meat in your spaghetti sauce.

Sustainable Storage:
Lasts up to 1 year.

Makes: 3 cups

Ingredients

2 cups dried minced onion

3 tablespoons dried oregano

2 tablespoons dried green bell pepper flakes

4 teaspoons dried basil

1 tablespoon dried minced garlic

4 teaspoons salt

4 tablespoons dried parsley

2 teaspoons dried rosemary

2 teaspoons dried thyme

2 teaspoons dried marjoram

Mix all spices together in a blender or food processor. Store in an airtight container in a cool, dark area.

Old Bay Seasoning

Your self-sufficiency should include your own seasonings! Try adding a little dried lemon peel to this mix. It adds the perfect flavor when you use it to season fish.

Sustainable Storage:
Lasts up to 3 years.

Makes: $\frac{1}{4}$ cup

Ingredients

1 tablespoon ground dried bay leaves

$2\frac{1}{2}$ teaspoons celery seeds

$\frac{1}{2}$ teaspoon mustard powder

$1\frac{1}{2}$ teaspoons freshly ground black pepper

$\frac{3}{4}$ teaspoon ground nutmeg

$\frac{1}{2}$ teaspoon ground cloves

$\frac{1}{2}$ teaspoon ground ginger

$\frac{1}{2}$ teaspoon paprika

$\frac{1}{2}$ teaspoon ground cayenne pepper

$\frac{1}{4}$ teaspoon ground mace

$\frac{1}{4}$ teaspoon ground cardamom

Add all ingredients to a 1-pint Mason jar. Put on lid and screw band, and shake until well combined. Store in jar with a tight-fitting lid in a cool, dark area.

Herbes de Provence

Keep spices from all over the world to make a diverse range of preserved foods! This spice blend comes from southern France, where people use it to flavor their food much as we use salt and pepper. Try some on your next chicken cookout for an amazing flavor and aroma.

Sustainable Storage:
Lasts up to 3 years.

Makes: $1\frac{1}{4}$ cups

Ingredients

2 tablespoons dried basil

4 teaspoons dried oregano

2 teaspoons dried marjoram

2 teaspoons dried tarragon

2 teaspoons dried thyme

2 teaspoons dried savory

$1\frac{1}{2}$ teaspoons dried crushed bay leaves

1 teaspoon fennel seeds

1 teaspoon dried mint

1 teaspoon ground sage

1 teaspoon dried rosemary

1 teaspoon dried lavender

Mix all spices together in a blender or food processor. Store in an airtight container in a cool, dark area.

Greek Seasoning Blend

Preserve this blend for a perfect beef or chicken seasoning. This mix can also become the base of a fantastic marinade; just add chicken or beef broth and vinegar.

Sustainable Storage:
Lasts up to 3 years.

Makes: 1 1/4 cups

Ingredients

6 tablespoons dried Greek oregano

1 1/2 tablespoons dried spearmint

2 teaspoons dried parsley flakes

2 tablespoons garlic powder

2 tablespoons onion powder

1 1/2 teaspoons salt

2 teaspoons cornstarch

2 teaspoons freshly ground black pepper

1/4 teaspoon ground nutmeg

1/4 teaspoon ground cinnamon

2 teaspoons beef bouillon granules

1. Rub oregano, spearmint, and parsley flakes between the palms of your hands over a small bowl.

2. Add remaining ingredients to the bowl and whisk until well combined.

3. Store in an airtight container in a cool, dark area.

Mexican Seasoning

As the name implies, this is a foundational spice blend for Spanish and Mexican dishes. You can also preserve and keep it for any dish that needs an extra kick. Try adding it to soups and stews for a hint of hot.

Sustainable Storage:
Lasts up to 3 years.

Makes: 4 tablespoons

Ingredients

2 tablespoons paprika

2 teaspoons ground dried oregano

1 teaspoon ground cumin

1 teaspoon ground turmeric

1 teaspoon garlic powder

1/4 teaspoon ground cayenne pepper

Mix all spices together in a blender or food processor. Store in an airtight container in a cool, dark area.

Italian Seasoning

Kitchen gardens are common in Italy, where people prefer fresh herbs for cooking. If you have your own garden, you can preserve and store this blend from fresh herbs. Just add extra-virgin olive oil, and freeze the mix.

Sustainable Storage:
Lasts up to 3 years in an airtight container and up to 1 year frozen.

Makes: 1 cup

Ingredients

1/3 cup dried oregano

1/3 cup dried basil

2 tablespoons dried rosemary

1/4 cup dried thyme

1 tablespoon garlic powder

1/4 cup dried minced onion

Mix all spices together in a blender or food processor. Store in an airtight container in a cool, dark area.

Herb and Spice Blends

These specific Herb and Spice Blends complement their respective meats perfectly.

Sustainable Storage:
Lasts up to 3 years.

Makes: $\frac{1}{3}$ cup of each blend

Ingredients for Beef

1 tablespoon coarsely ground
    black pepper

1 tablespoon crushed red
    pepper flakes

$2\frac{1}{2}$ tablespoons garlic powder

1 tablespoon dried minced onion

Ingredients for Fish

2 tablespoons dried dill

2 tablespoons dried crushed
    bay leaves

2 tablespoons freeze-dried
    chives

Ingredients for Vegetables

2 tablespoons dried thyme

2 tablespoons dried oregano

2 tablespoons dried basil

Ingredients for Chicken

2 tablespoons curry powder

2 tablespoons paprika

2 tablespoons dried lemon peel

Ingredients for Lamb

$1\frac{1}{2}$ tablespoons dried marjoram

1 tablespoon dried rosemary

1 tablespoon ground white pepper

2 tablespoons garlic powder

For each herb blend, put all ingredients into a blender or food processor; process until fine. Store in an airtight container in a cool, dark area.

Preservation Pointers

These Herb and Spice Blends are designed to bring out the flavors of specific meats or vegetables. However, you can try adding a little of your own favorite herbs or spices to the mixes to suit your tastes. You can also try using the beef blend with chicken or the fish blend with vegetables.

CHAPTER THIRTEEN

Jams, Jellies, Conserves, and Marmalade

Maple Apple Jam

Who said preserving for self-sustainability couldn't be fun? As a surprise for your family, leave $\frac{1}{2}$" of space at the top of the jars and sprinkle hard-crack caramel and chopped nuts on top of the jam.

Sustainable Storage:
Lasts up to 2 years.

Makes: $8\frac{1}{2}$ pints

Ingredients

6 pounds mixed apples, chopped

6 cups granulated sugar

1 cup real maple syrup

$\frac{1}{2}$ teaspoon ground cinnamon

$\frac{1}{2}$ teaspoon ground allspice

$\frac{1}{2}$ teaspoon ground nutmeg

$\frac{1}{2}$ teaspoon ground ginger

$\frac{1}{4}$ teaspoon ground cloves

1 (1.75-ounce) box powdered fruit pectin

1. In a large nonreactive pot over medium-low heat, combine all ingredients. Bring to a boil.

2. Continue boiling, stirring frequently, until the jam holds its shape when put on a cold platter.

3. Pour hot jam into sterilized jars, leaving $\frac{1}{4}$" headspace at the top of each jar. Make sure to remove all air bubbles. Wipe rims and place sterilized lid on each jar. Tightly screw on sterilized screw bands, and process in a water-bath canner for 10 minutes.

4. Move the jars to a cooling surface, leaving plenty of space between the jars. Check all the lids when cool, tightening as needed. If any of the jars did not seal, refrigerate or freeze instead.

> **Preservation Pointers**
>
> Jams, jellies, and preserves are all made from fruit, sugar, and fruit pectin. So what makes them different? With jam, fruit pulp remains in the mix for a thicker but less solid final product. Fruit juice is used in jelly, and fruit chunks and syrup blend together to provide the unique texture of preserves.

Apple Pie Jelly

Can your own jellies for a sweet pick-me-up whenever you and your family want it! Try serving this hot with a drizzle of sweet cream on top.

Sustainable Storage: Lasts up to 2 years.

Makes: 6–7 pints

Ingredients

4 cups apple juice

4 tablespoons real maple syrup

3 teaspoons apple pie spice

1 (1.75-ounce) box powdered fruit pectin

5 cups granulated sugar

1. In a large stockpot over high heat, combine apple juice, maple syrup, and apple pie spice.

2. Add pectin and bring to a hard boil until it dissolves into the juice.

3. Slowly stir in sugar and bring back to a rolling boil over high heat. Boil for 1 full minute.

4. Remove from heat and skim off foam with a metal spoon. Ladle hot jelly into sterilized jars, leaving $1/4$" headspace at the top of each jar. Make sure to remove all air bubbles. Wipe rims and place sterilized lid on each jar. Tightly screw on sterilized screw bands, and process in a water-bath canner for 15 minutes.

5. Move the jars to a cooling surface, leaving plenty of space between the jars. Check all the lids when cool, tightening as needed. If any of the jars did not seal, refrigerate or freeze instead.

Garlic Jelly

Your preserved jellies don't always have to be sweet! Stock this different kind of jelly to be used as a condiment. It's wonderful added to a marinade or brushed directly on meat while cooking.

Sustainable Storage:
Lasts up to 1 year.

Makes: 5½ pints

Ingredients

¼ pound garlic, peeled

2 cups white vinegar, divided

5 cups granulated sugar

1 (3-ounce) pouch liquid fruit pectin

1. Using a food processor or blender, blend garlic and ½ cup vinegar until smooth.

2. In a large stockpot over high heat, combine garlic mixture, remaining 1½ cups vinegar, and sugar. Bring mixture to a boil, stirring constantly.

3. Quickly stir in pectin; return to a boil and boil hard 1 minute, stirring constantly.

4. Remove from heat. Ladle hot jelly into sterilized jars, leaving ¼" headspace at the top of each jar. Make sure to remove all air bubbles. Wipe rims and place sterilized lid on each jar. Tightly screw on sterilized screw bands, and process in a water-bath canner for 10 minutes.

5. Move the jars to a cooling surface, leaving plenty of space between the jars. Check all the lids when cool, tightening as needed. If any of the jars did not seal, refrigerate or freeze instead.

Dandelion Jelly

What we consider a pesky weed has been preserved and used for centuries in cooking. Be very careful to get all the green parts off the flowers, or the result will be very bitter.

Sustainable Storage:
Lasts up to 2 years.

Makes: 2–3 pints

Ingredients

4 cups yellow parts of dandelion blossoms

3 cups boiling water

4½ cups granulated sugar

20 drops yellow food coloring

2 tablespoons fresh lemon juice

1 (3-ounce) box powdered fruit pectin

1. In a large saucepan over low heat, combine the flowers and boiling water; simmer for 10 minutes. The flowers must be covered with water; if there are too many, break this step into batches. Warning: If the water begins to boil, the flavor of this jelly really suffers.

2. Strain the water, extracting as much of the juice from the flowers as possible. Make sure your final measure is 3 cups juice; add water if needed.

3. Return juice to saucepan and bring to a boil over medium heat. Add sugar, food coloring, and lemon juice. Add pectin and boil for 1 more minute.

4. Pour hot jelly into sterilized jars, leaving ¼" headspace at the top of each jar. Make sure to remove all air bubbles. Wipe rims and place sterilized lid on each jar. Tightly screw on sterilized screw bands, and process in a water-bath canner for 10 minutes.

5. Move the jars to a cooling surface, leaving plenty of space between the jars. Check all the lids when cool, tightening as needed. If any of the jars did not seal, refrigerate or freeze instead.

Lemon Lime Marmalade

Stock up on this great Lemon Lime Marmalade, which can double as a fish and poultry marinade if you blend it with a little vinegar to offset the sweetness.

Sustainable Storage:
Lasts up to 2 years.

Makes: 6 pints

Ingredients

5 medium lemons

6 medium limes

8 cups water

8 cups granulated sugar

½ cup candied ginger

1. Cut lemons and limes in half and squeeze out juice; reserve juice.

2. Remove citrus peel in thin strips, avoiding bitter white pith.

3. In a large saucepan over medium heat, combine citrus skins, juice, and water. Bring to a boil; simmer until skins are tender, about 15 minutes.

4. Add sugar and ginger, stirring constantly; boil again until mixture reaches 220°F.

5. Pour hot marmalade into sterilized jars, leaving ¼" headspace at the top of each jar. Make sure to remove all air bubbles. Wipe rims and place sterilized lid on each jar. Tightly screw on sterilized screw bands, and process in a water-bath canner for 10 minutes.

6. Move the jars to a cooling surface, leaving plenty of space between the jars. Check all the lids when cool, tightening as needed. If any of the jars did not seal, refrigerate or freeze instead.

Cantaloupe Conserve

This Cantaloupe Conserve is a sweet treat you can preserve and enjoy year-round. Cantaloupe can be tricky to cook with, so follow this recipe carefully.

Sustainable Storage:
Lasts up to 2 years.

Makes: $7\frac{1}{2}$ pints

Ingredients

6 pounds cantaloupe, peeled, seeded, and cut into $\frac{1}{2}$" cubes

8 cups granulated sugar

2 teaspoons freshly grated lemon zest

$\frac{1}{2}$ cup fresh lemon juice

2 cups golden raisins

$1\frac{1}{2}$ cups toasted chopped almonds

$\frac{1}{4}$ teaspoon almond extract

1. In a very large bowl, toss cantaloupe with sugar. Cover with plastic wrap; leave standing at room temperature 8–10 hours.

2. In a large stockpot over medium heat, combine cantaloupe with remaining ingredients except almonds and almond extract. Bring to a boil; cook until mixture starts to thicken, 15–20 minutes. Stir constantly.

3. Remove from heat; stir in almonds and almond extract. Quickly skim off foam with a metal spoon.

4. Ladle conserve into sterilized jars, leaving $\frac{1}{2}$" headspace at the top of each jar. Make sure to remove all air bubbles. Wipe rims and place sterilized lid on each jar. Tightly screw on sterilized screw bands, and process in a water-bath canner for 10 minutes.

5. Move the jars to a cooling surface, leaving plenty of space between the jars. Check all the lids when cool, tightening as needed. If any of the jars did not seal, refrigerate or freeze instead.

Blackberry Preserves

This recipe is flexible; use your foraged berries, or head to the farmers' market for raspberries, if you prefer.

Sustainable Storage:
Lasts up to 2 years.

Makes: about 6 pints

Ingredients

3 quarts fully ripe blackberries

7½ cups granulated sugar

½ cup water

2 (3-ounce) pouches liquid fruit pectin

1. Place blackberries into a large stockpot. Crush with a potato masher to extract juice. Stir in the sugar and mix well. Add water.

2. Bring to a full rolling boil over high heat, stirring constantly.

3. Add pectin and return to a full rolling boil. Boil hard for 1 minute. Remove from heat.

4. Skim off foam. Ladle hot preserves into sterilized jars, leaving ¼" headspace at the top of each jar. Make sure to remove all air bubbles. Wipe rims and place sterilized lid on each jar. Tightly screw on sterilized screw bands, and process in a water-bath canner for 5 minutes.

5. Move the jars to a cooling surface, leaving plenty of space between the jars. Check all the lids when cool, tightening as needed. If any of the jars did not seal, refrigerate or freeze.

Fig Walnut Conserve

You'll never settle for boring store-bought conserves again. Try this Fig Walnut Conserve warm on bread to release its great aroma.

Sustainable Storage:
Lasts up to 1 year.

Makes: 6 pints

Ingredients

5 pounds dried figs

6 cups granulated sugar

⅛ teaspoon ground cinnamon

⅛ teaspoon ground allspice

⅛ teaspoon ground cardamom

⅛ teaspoon ground ginger

¾ cup apple juice

¼ cup fresh lemon juice

1 cup chopped walnuts

1. In a large heatproof bowl, cover figs with boiling water; let stand 10 minutes. Drain, then stem and chop figs.

2. In a large saucepan over low heat, combine figs with sugar, cinnamon, allspice, cardamom, ginger, and apple juice. Bring slowly to a boil; stir until sugar dissolves. Cook rapidly until thickened. Stir frequently to prevent sticking.

3. Add lemon juice; cook for 1 minute longer. Remove from heat and stir in walnuts.

4. Ladle hot conserve into sterilized jars, leaving ¼" headspace at the top of each jar. Make sure to remove all air bubbles. Wipe rims and place sterilized lid on each jar. Tightly screw on sterilized screw bands, and process in a water-bath canner for 15 minutes.

5. Move the jars to a cooling surface, leaving plenty of space between the jars. Check all the lids when cool, tightening as needed. If any of the jars did not seal, refrigerate or freeze instead.

Very Cherry

Some people preserve and store this jam with cinnamon, allspice, or cloves. If you want to add spices, about $\frac{1}{2}$ teaspoon each does the trick.

Sustainable Storage: Lasts up to 2 years.

Makes: 3 pints

Ingredients

1 quart Bing cherries, pitted and chopped

1 (3-ounce) box powdered fruit pectin

$\frac{1}{4}$ cup fresh lemon juice

$\frac{1}{4}$ cup cherry liqueur

$4\frac{1}{2}$ cups granulated sugar

1. In a large saucepan over medium heat, combine all ingredients except sugar.

2. Bring to a boil, stirring regularly. Add sugar; continue stirring until completely dissolved. Continue boiling for 2 minutes after sugar dissolves.

3. Ladle hot jam into sterilized jars, leaving $\frac{1}{4}$" headspace at the top of each jar. Make sure to remove all air bubbles. Wipe rims and place sterilized lid on each jar. Tightly screw on sterilized screw bands, and process in a water-bath canner for 10 minutes.

4. Move the jars to a cooling surface, leaving plenty of space between the jars. Check all the lids when cool, tightening as needed. If any of the jars did not seal, refrigerate or freeze instead.

Prickly Pear Cactus Marmalade

While oranges are the most popular fruit for marmalade, your preserving shouldn't be limited! The prickly pear packs a very pleasant and flavorful surprise.

Sustainable Storage:
Lasts up to 2 years.

Makes: 6½ pints

Ingredients

3 cups peeled, seeded, and chopped oranges

1 cup thinly sliced lemon

4 cups water

4 cups peeled, seeded, and chopped prickly pears

6 cups granulated sugar

2 tablespoons freshly grated lemon zest

1. In a large saucepan over low heat, combine oranges, lemon, and water. Simmer for 5 minutes. Remove from heat and cover. Let stand 12–18 hours in refrigerator.

2. Stir in prickly pears; add sugar and lemon zest. Return saucepan to medium-low heat. Bring to a boil, stirring until sugar dissolves. Cook rapidly until gelling point is reached (220°F).

3. As mixture thickens, stir frequently to prevent sticking. Remove from heat. Skim foam from the top if necessary.

4. Ladle hot marmalade into sterilized jars, leaving ¼" headspace at the top of each jar. Make sure to remove all air bubbles. Wipe rims and place sterilized lid on each jar. Tightly screw on sterilized screw bands, and process in a water-bath canner for 15 minutes.

5. Move the jars to a cooling surface, leaving plenty of space between the jars. Check all the lids when cool, tightening as needed. If any of the jars did not seal, refrigerate or freeze.

Apricot Raspberry Jam

Add your favorite chopped nuts for a personal and sustainable twist! Use as a spread or as a tart filling.

Sustainable Storage:
Lasts up to 2 years.

Makes: 7½ pints

Ingredients

2 pounds fresh apricots, peeled and pitted

1 pint raspberries

6 cups granulated sugar

¼ cup fresh lemon juice

1 teaspoon freshly grated lemon zest

1 tablespoon unsalted butter

1 (3-ounce) pouch liquid fruit pectin

1. In a large stockpot, combine apricots and raspberries. Crush with a potato masher.

2. Stir in sugar, lemon juice, lemon zest, and butter. Bring to a boil over high heat, stirring constantly.

3. Cook for 15 minutes until mixture starts to thicken, stirring constantly. Add pectin.

4. Bring to a rolling boil and boil for 1 minute, stirring constantly.

5. Ladle hot jam into sterilized jars, leaving ¼" headspace at the top of each jar. Make sure to remove all air bubbles. Wipe rims and place sterilized lid on each jar. Tightly screw on sterilized screw bands, and process in a water-bath canner for 15 minutes.

6. Move the jars to a cooling surface, leaving plenty of space between the jars. Check all the lids when cool, tightening as needed. If any of the jars did not seal, refrigerate or freeze instead.

Brandied Plum Jam

Preserve this jam with different types of brandies for a varied stock of plum jams!

Sustainable Storage:
Lasts up to 2 years.

Makes: 4 pints

Ingredients

4 pounds plums, pitted and chopped

$3/4$ cup water

2 tablespoons fresh lemon juice

1 (1.75-ounce) box powdered fruit pectin

7 cups granulated sugar

1 cup blackberry brandy

1. In a large stockpot over high heat, combine plums, water, lemon juice, and pectin. Bring to a rolling boil, stirring constantly.

2. Add sugar and return to a rolling boil. Boil hard for 1 minute, stirring constantly.

3. Remove from heat and stir in brandy.

4. Ladle hot jam into sterilized jars, leaving $1/4$" headspace at the top of each jar. Make sure to remove all air bubbles. Wipe rims and place sterilized lid on each jar. Tightly screw on sterilized screw bands, and process in a water-bath canner for 10 minutes.

5. Move the jars to a cooling surface, leaving plenty of space between the jars. Check all the lids when cool, tightening as needed. If any of the jars did not seal, refrigerate or freeze instead.

Butterscotch Peach Preserves

You'll be glad you stocked these Butterscotch Peach Preserves in your pantry. It's wonderful for tarts or over ice cream!

Sustainable Storage:
Lasts up to 2 years.

Makes: 2½–3 pints

Ingredients

6 cups peeled, pitted, and chopped peaches

⅓ cup fresh lemon juice

5 cups firmly packed dark brown sugar

1. In a large stockpot, combine peaches and lemon juice. Crush fruit with a potato masher. Bring to a boil over medium heat; reduce heat to low. Cover and simmer for 10 minutes, stirring occasionally.

2. Stir in brown sugar. Increase heat to medium-high and cook for 20–25 minutes, until slightly thickened. Stir often.

3. Remove from heat and stir jam for 3–5 minutes. Skim off foam if necessary.

4. Ladle hot preserves into sterilized jars, leaving ¼" headspace at the top of each jar. Make sure to remove all air bubbles. Wipe rims and place sterilized lid on each jar. Tightly screw on sterilized screw bands, and process in a water-bath canner for 10 minutes.

5. Move the jars to a cooling surface, leaving plenty of space between the jars. Check all the lids when cool, tightening as needed. If any of the jars did not seal, refrigerate or freeze instead.

Pomegranate Jelly

Not only does this jelly taste great, but it's also rich in antioxidants and vitamins A, C, and E.

Sustainable Storage:
Lasts up to 2 years.

Makes: 3½ pints

Ingredients

3½ cups pomegranate juice

2 tablespoons fresh lemon juice

6 cups granulated sugar

1 (3-ounce) pouch liquid fruit pectin

1. In a large nonreactive saucepan over medium heat, combine pomegranate juice, lemon juice, and sugar.

2. Bring to a full rolling boil, stirring regularly. Stir in pectin and continue to boil for 1 minute.

3. Ladle hot jelly into sterilized jars, leaving ¼" headspace at the top of each jar. Make sure to remove all air bubbles. Wipe rims and place sterilized lid on each jar. Tightly screw on sterilized screw bands, and process in a water-bath canner for 10 minutes.

4. Move the jars to a cooling surface, leaving plenty of space between the jars. Check all the lids when cool, tightening as needed. If any of the jars did not seal, refrigerate or freeze instead.

Pineapple Strawberry Delight

Preserve your summer strawberries with this Pineapple Strawberry Delight. One cup of strawberries provides 140 percent of the daily recommended amount of vitamin C. This fruit also fights bad cholesterol.

Sustainable Storage:
Lasts up to 2 years.

Makes: 8½ pints

Ingredients

1 pound strawberries, hulled and sliced

2⅓ cups crushed pineapple with juice

5 cups granulated sugar

3 tablespoons fresh lemon juice

1 teaspoon freshly grated lemon zest

1 (3-ounce) pouch liquid fruit pectin

1. In a large stockpot over medium heat, combine strawberries and pineapple with juice. Bring to a boil, stirring frequently.

2. Stir in sugar, lemon juice, and lemon zest. Raise heat to high and return to a boil, stirring constantly.

3. Cook for 15 minutes until mixture starts to thicken, stirring constantly. Add pectin. Return to a rolling boil and boil for 1 minute, stirring constantly.

4. Ladle hot preserves into sterilized jars, leaving ¼" headspace at the top of each jar. Make sure to remove all air bubbles. Wipe rims and place sterilized lid on each jar. Tightly screw on sterilized screw bands, and process in a water-bath canner for 10 minutes.

5. Move the jars to a cooling surface, leaving plenty of space between the jars. Check all the lids when cool, tightening as needed. If any of the jars did not seal, refrigerate or freeze instead.

Jeanne's Elder-Blueberry Jam

Some studies indicate that elderberries may help the body recuperate from the flu. Preserve this jam to keep for when you're feeling under the weather.

Sustainable Storage: Lasts up to 2 years.

Makes: about 7 pints

Ingredients

1 quart crushed elderberries

1 quart crushed blueberries

6 cups granulated sugar

$\frac{1}{4}$ cup white vinegar

2 teaspoons dried orange zest

2 teaspoons vanilla extract

1. In a large stockpot over medium heat, combine all ingredients. Slowly bring to a boil, stirring until sugar dissolves. Continue to boil until thick, stirring frequently to prevent sticking.

2. Ladle hot jam into sterilized jars, leaving $\frac{1}{4}$" headspace at the top of each jar. Make sure to remove all air bubbles. Wipe rims and place sterilized lid on each jar. Tightly screw on sterilized screw bands, and process in a water-bath canner for 10 minutes.

3. Move the jars to a cooling surface, leaving plenty of space between the jars. Check all the lids when cool, tightening as needed. If any of the jars did not seal, refrigerate or freeze instead.

Purple Plum Preserves

Your family will thank you for stocking these Purple Plum Preserves in the pantry. Honey and mace make the plums yummy.

Sustainable Storage:
Lasts up to 2 years.

Makes: 5 pints

Ingredients

5 pounds purple plums, pitted and chopped

7 cups granulated sugar

1 cup honey

½ cup fresh lemon juice

1½ cups water

1 teaspoon ground mace

1. In a large stockpot over medium heat, combine all ingredients. Bring slowly to a boil, stirring until sugar dissolves.

2. Cook for 15 minutes, until mixture thickens, stirring occasionally to prevent sticking.

3. Ladle hot preserves into sterilized jars, leaving ¼" headspace at the top of each jar. Make sure to remove all air bubbles. Wipe rims and place sterilized lid on each jar. Tightly screw on sterilized screw bands, and process in a water-bath canner for 15 minutes.

4. Move the jars to a cooling surface, leaving plenty of space between the jars. Check all the lids when cool, tightening as needed. If any of the jars did not seal, refrigerate or freeze instead.

Raspberry Surprise Preserves

No one will guess that there are beets in this scrumptious condiment. Preserve this recipe for a creative way to get picky children to eat the vegetable. The color is a bright red and the flavor is delightful.

Sustainable Storage:
Lasts up to 2 years.

Makes: about 7 pints

Ingredients

10 pounds large beets

1/2 cup fresh lemon juice

2 teaspoons dried lemon peel

2 (1.75-ounce) boxes powdered fruit pectin

5 cups granulated sugar

2 (3-ounce) packages raspberry gelatin

1. In a large stockpot, cook beets in enough water to cover until tender. Remove from stockpot with a slotted spoon, reserving cooking liquid. When beets are cool, peel, cut into chunks, and purée in a food processor or blender.

2. Measure 7½ cups of the reserved cooking liquid. Add water to make the full amount if necessary.

3. In a large stockpot over medium-high heat, combine puréed beets, reserved cooking liquid, lemon juice, lemon peel, and pectin. Stir well and bring to a boil.

4. Add sugar and packaged gelatin. Boil for 8–10 minutes, stirring frequently to prevent scorching. Skim off foam, if necessary.

5. Ladle preserves into sterilized jars, leaving 1/4" headspace at the top of each jar. Make sure to remove all air bubbles. Wipe rims and place sterilized lid on each jar. Tightly screw on sterilized screw bands, and process in a water-bath canner for 10 minutes.

6. Move the jars to a cooling surface, leaving plenty of space between the jars. Check all the lids when cool, tightening as needed. If any of the jars did not seal, refrigerate or freeze instead.

Wild Strawberry Preserves

Preserving this classic recipe transports you from your kitchen to the countryside every time you open the lid.

Sustainable Storage: Lasts up to 1 year when canned or frozen.

Makes: 8 half-pints

Ingredients

4 cups ripe strawberries, hulled and mashed

4 cups granulated sugar

1 tablespoon fresh lemon juice

1. In a medium bowl, combine strawberries and sugar. Let sit at room temperature for about 1 hour, until they begin getting juicy.

2. Transfer strawberry mixture to a large saucepan over medium heat. Add lemon juice and bring to a full rolling boil. Continue to boil for 7 minutes, stirring constantly.

3. Pour hot preserves into 8 sterilized half-pint jars, leaving $\frac{1}{4}$" headspace at the top of each jar. Make sure to remove all air bubbles. Wipe rims and place sterilized lid on each jar. Tightly screw on sterilized screw bands, and process in a water-bath canner for 10 minutes.

4. Move the jars to a cooling surface, leaving plenty of space between the jars. Check all the lids when cool, tightening as needed. If any of the jars did not seal, refrigerate or freeze instead.

Persimmon Jam

It's vital that you preserve ripe persimmons in this jam or it will be very tart. Buy and test the fruit during its peak season, and give it time if it isn't ripe yet.

Sustainable Storage:
Lasts up to 2 years.

Makes: 7 cups

Ingredients
5 cups persimmon purée
3 cups granulated sugar
$\frac{1}{4}$ cup fresh lemon juice
$\frac{1}{2}$ teaspoon freshly grated lemon zest
$\frac{1}{8}$ teaspoon ground nutmeg
$\frac{1}{8}$ teaspoon ground cloves

1. In large nonreactive saucepan over medium heat, combine all ingredients. Bring to a boil; cook for 30 minutes, stirring regularly.

2. Cool and transfer into freezer-safe containers, leaving $\frac{1}{4}$" headspace for expansion. Leave out overnight before freezing.

Fruit Punch Jelly

This recipe is very fast and easy, and you can use any soft drink mix you wish. Freeze for a sweet and refreshing treat when you want it!

Sustainable Storage:
Lasts up to 1 year.

Makes: about 4 cups

Ingredients
1 envelope unsweetened mixed-fruit soft drink mix
3 cups water
3 cups granulated sugar
1 (1.75-ounce) box powdered fruit pectin

1. In a medium saucepan over medium heat, dissolve drink mix in water. Bring to a boil, stirring constantly.

2. In a medium bowl, combine sugar with pectin. Add to drink mixture slowly, and boil for 1 more minute.

3. Cool slightly, then transfer into freezer containers, leaving $\frac{1}{2}$" headspace for expansion. Let sit overnight before freezing.

Mango Madness

This is a lovely, fresh jam, perfect for a hot summer day. Or save it for a chilly winter morning while reminiscing about summer.

Sustainable Storage:
Lasts up to 1 year.

Makes: about 6 cups

Ingredients

3 cups mashed ripe mangoes

¼ cup fresh lemon juice

5 cups granulated sugar

½ cup water

¼ cup mango or passion fruit juice

1 (1.75-ounce) box powdered fruit pectin

1. In a large bowl, combine mangoes with lemon juice and sugar. Let sit for 15 minutes.

2. In a large saucepan over medium heat, combine water, mango juice, and pectin. Bring to a boil; boil for 1 minute.

3. Add fruit mixture and continue boiling for 3 minutes, until sugar dissolves.

4. Cool and transfer into freezer-safe containers, leaving ½" headspace for expansion. Let sit for 24 hours before freezing.

Plumberry Jam

Experiment with your sustainable home preserving and use what you have already! You can substitute 1 cup blueberries for strawberries.

Sustainable Storage:
Lasts up to 3 months in the refrigerator or up to 1 year in the freezer.

Makes: 4 pints

Ingredients

2 cups red raspberries

1 cup hulled strawberries

1 cup peeled, pitted, and diced ripe plums

5 cups granulated sugar

½ cup light corn syrup

¾ cup water

1 (3-ounce) box powdered fruit pectin

1. In a large bowl, combine raspberries, strawberries, and plums with sugar. Let stand for 15 minutes.

2. In a saucepan over medium heat, combine fruit with corn syrup and water. Bring to a boil.

3. Add pectin and continue boiling for 1 minute. Cool and put into containers. This can be refrigerated or frozen; if freezing, leave ½" headspace for expansion.

Perfect Peaches and Pears

Some recipes for preserving freezer jelly use cornstarch as a thickener. Cornstarch, however, lends the jelly a completely different texture, so this recipe relies on pectin.

Sustainable Storage:
Lasts up to 3 months.

Makes: 10 cups

Ingredients

3 ripe (not mushy) pears, peeled, cored, and diced

3 small ripe peaches, peeled, pitted, and diced

1 teaspoon orange juice

1 teaspoon freshly grated orange zest

1 teaspoon freshly grated lemon zest

1 tablespoon grated fresh ginger

2 cups granulated sugar

2 cups water

1 (1.75-ounce) box powdered fruit pectin

1. In a large saucepan over medium-low heat, combine pears, peaches, orange juice, orange zest, lemon zest, and ginger. Cook until fruit is fully tender.

2. Add sugar and water and bring to a boil. Cook for 15 minutes. Add pectin and boil for 1 minute more. Remove from heat.

3. Cool and transfer into freezer-safe containers, leaving $\frac{1}{2}$" headspace for expansion.

Banana Jam

This is a sustainable way to use up bananas that are just about to be overripe. If you want other spices in the mix, add some allspice or cinnamon.

Sustainable Storage:
Lasts up to 1 week.

Makes: 6 cups

Ingredients

6 ripe bananas, peeled and sliced

½ cup firmly packed light brown sugar

2 tablespoons grated fresh ginger

⅔ cup citrus juice

1. In a large saucepan over low heat, combine all ingredients. Cook, stirring regularly, for 2 hours. Or, to avoid stirring, cook in a slow cooker on low heat for 5 hours.

2. Cool and put into jars, and store in refrigerator.

Pineapple Rhubarb Jam

Look for crisp, young rhubarb that's firm and brightly colored to preserve this delicious Pineapple Rhubarb Jam.

Sustainable Storage:
Lasts up to 3 months.

Makes: about 6 cups

Ingredients

5 cups diced rhubarb

5 cups granulated sugar

1 cup water

1 cup crushed pineapple, drained

1 (3-ounce) box powdered fruit pectin

1. In a large saucepan over medium heat, combine rhubarb, sugar, and water. Bring to a boil and boil for 15 minutes. Reduce heat to low and add pineapple; simmer another 10 minutes.

2. Add pectin and mix well. Cool and put into jars, storing in the refrigerator for immediate use.

GLOSSARY

Alum
Until recently, a common ingredient in pickling recipes. It has been found to cause stomach problems.

Antioxidant
Keeps food from browning. Examples include lemon and lime juice.

Bacteria
Organisms that may be harmful if not destroyed properly. Any low-acid recipes must be processed in a pressure canner to 250°F for a specific length of time.

Blanch
A fast bath in boiling water, usually followed by an ice- or cold-water bath. Prepares many fruits and vegetables for preserving.

Boiling-water canning
Process requiring jars to be completely immersed in boiling water for a set length of time in order to bring the food to 212°F and create a vacuum seal on the lids.

Botulism
Food poisoning caused by the botulinum toxin, which may grow in foods that haven't been properly processed (allowing bacteria to reproduce). Canning and preserving methods strive to eliminate these toxins by removing air and using acids and high temperatures to kill spores.

Brine
A mixture consisting primarily of salt and water, used in pickling.

Candying
Encrusting with sugar, often through the use of boiling syrup. A common method of preserving fruit rinds and ginger for baking purposes.

Canning and pickling salt
A fine salt with no iodine or anticaking ingredients that can discolor vegetables.

Cheesecloth
A cloth used to strain pulp or juice, especially for jelly making. It's also useful as a container for spices during pickling, which can then be discarded before pickles are put in jars.

Chutney
A slow-cooked blend of fruit, vegetables, spices, and/or vinegar.

Cold pack
A canning process in which fruits and vegetables go into the jar raw. Afterward, some type of canning liquid is added (usually hot) and the jars are processed.

Conserve
Jamlike spread, often using two or more fruits, and possibly including nuts.

Crisping agent
A commercial product consisting of calcium chloride, sold under the brand name Pickle Crisp. Used to keep pickles fresh in lieu of alum.

Dial gauge
Part of a pressure canner that shows what pressure level the canner has reached.

Fermentation
A method of preserving food by introducing yeasts. Unanticipated fermentation can indicate other micro-organisms that can cause sickness.

Gelling point
A temperature of 220°F, at which point various liquids gel.

Headspace

Amount of room left between the top of the food and the lid in a canning jar. This room is necessary to create a vacuum seal.

High-acid food

Food with a pH value of 4.6 or less, such as tomatoes and many fruit juices. These foods can be processed using boiling-water methods.

Hot pack

A form of canning where food goes into the jars hot to be processed.

Jam

Crushed fruit and sugar (sometimes nuts) processed together into a spread.

Jelly

A firm spread made from juice and sugar, to which pectin may be added.

Low-acid food

Foods with a pH higher than 4.6. Examples include most seafood, meat, and vegetables. These foods must be pressure canned, heated to 250°F.

Marmalade

A spread that includes fruit and peel pieces mingled into a jelly base.

Pectin

A fruit and vegetable carbohydrate frequently used to make jelly, jam, and other spreads.

Pickling

A preservation process that uses vinegar with spices and water. Foods are processed in boiling-water canners.

Preserves

A spread that preserves fruit in sugar syrup. The fruit retains its shape.

Pressure canning
A process used on low-acid foods that cooks them to 250°F throughout, killing bacteria.

Processing
Heating canning jars to specific temperatures for a specific amount of time to kill bacteria, mold, and yeast. Also creates the vacuum seal on canned foods.

Raw pack
Filling jars with unheated meat or fish prior to processing.

Relish
A blend of diced vegetables or fruits in a seasoned vinegar solution.

Reprocessing
Removing and reheating the lid, cleaning and reheating the jar, and reheating the food inside the jar according to the recipe, followed by processing again. This method is used when a canning jar doesn't seal properly.

Smoke curing
A way of preserving food by smoking it. Also adds flavor to the preserved item.

Syrup
A blend of sugar and other liquids used to cover ingredients in a jar before processing.

Venting
Heating of canning jars to force the air out.

Weighted gauge
A gauge on pressure canners consisting of weights, normally for 5, 10, and 15 pounds of pressure, which go on top of a valve. When the weight rocks, the right pressure has been achieved.

US/METRIC CONVERSION CHART

Volume Conversions

US Volume Measure	Metric Equivalent
1/8 teaspoon	0.5 milliliter
1/4 teaspoon	1 milliliter
1/2 teaspoon	2 milliliters
1 teaspoon	5 milliliters
1/2 tablespoon	7 milliliters
1 tablespoon (3 teaspoons)	15 milliliters
2 tablespoons (1 fluid ounce)	30 milliliters
1/4 cup (4 tablespoons)	60 milliliters
1/3 cup	90 milliliters
1/2 cup (4 fluid ounces)	125 milliliters
2/3 cup	160 milliliters
3/4 cup (6 fluid ounces)	180 milliliters
1 cup (16 tablespoons)	250 milliliters
1 pint (2 cups)	500 milliliters
1 quart (4 cups)	1 liter (about)

Weight Conversions

US Weight Measure	Metric Equivalent
1/2 ounce	15 grams
1 ounce	30 grams
2 ounces	60 grams
3 ounces	85 grams
1/4 pound (4 ounces)	115 grams
1/2 pound (8 ounces)	225 grams
3/4 pound (12 ounces)	340 grams
1 pound (16 ounces)	454 grams

Oven Temperature Conversions

Degrees Fahrenheit	Degrees Celsius
200 degrees F	95 degrees C
250 degrees F	120 degrees C
275 degrees F	135 degrees C
300 degrees F	150 degrees C
325 degrees F	160 degrees C
350 degrees F	180 degrees C
375 degrees F	190 degrees C
400 degrees F	205 degrees C
425 degrees F	220 degrees C
450 degrees F	230 degrees C

Baking Pan Sizes

American	Metric
8 x 1 1/2 inch round baking pan	20 x 4 cm cake tin
9 x 1 1/2 inch round baking pan	23 x 3.5 cm cake tin
11 x 7 x 1 1/2 inch baking pan	28 x 18 x 4 cm baking tin
13 x 9 x 2 inch baking pan	30 x 20 x 5 cm baking tin
2 quart rectangular baking dish	30 x 20 x 3 cm baking tin
15 x 10 x 2 inch baking pan	30 x 25 x 2 cm baking tin (Swiss roll tin)
9 inch pie plate	22 x 4 or 23 x 4 cm pie plate
7 or 8 inch springform pan	18 or 20 cm springform or loose bottom cake tin
9 x 5 x 3 inch loaf pan	23 x 13 x 7 cm or 2 lb narrow loaf or pâté tin
1 1/2 quart casserole	1.5 liter casserole
2 quart casserole	2 liter casserole

INDEX

Note: Page numbers in **bold** indicate recipe category lists.